Hagi Kenaan is Professor of Philosophy at Tel Aviv University. He works in the areas of continental philosophy, phenomenology, aesthetics and the philosophy of art. He is the author of *The Present Personal: Philosophy and the Hidden Face of Language* (Columbia University Press, 2005) and co-editor of *Philosophy's Moods: The Affective Grounds of Thinking* (Springer, 2011).

'Kenaan's brilliant study reveals what Levinas' "ethical turn" has to teach us about the ethical potential of the visual. His study offers nothing less than a guide for restoring to us an ethics of vision in our postmodern world. It is an urgent, compelling and, ultimately, hopeful work.'
Martin Berger, Professor and Chair, History of Art and Visual Culture, University of California at Santa Cruz

'Hagi Kenaan questions the manner in which the Other's face shows itself to us. Reading Levinas in light of the philosophies of Husserl, Heidegger, Merleau-Ponty and Sartre, he analyses with finesse how the face subverts the primacy of consciousness. The face is a reminder of an alterity irreducible to the flow of images that tyrannically occupy our field of vision ... To see a face is not to see a phenomenon, but to hear a call addressing me. It is in this difficult, paradoxical and eminently singular optics that ethics upholds itself. Ethics becomes an optics when the vulnerability of the face is perceived as a call for a conversion of the gaze.'
Catherine Chalier, Professor of Philosophy, University of Paris X – Nanterre

'*The Ethics of Visuality* is an extraordinary achievement. The author offers a brilliant meditation not only on Levinas' thought but also through it, engaging and going beyond it, culminating in profound insights ... Kenaan here builds on his own thought-provoking work – namely, on the presence of the singular in language and the challenges it raises. Levinas, as is well known, raises similar questions in his conception of alterity and the primacy of the ethical. Kenaan's achievement in this book is both an elaboration of Levinas' thought through an exploration of his claim that 'ethics is an optics' and a critical evaluation of Levinas' work through bringing the tension between optics and alterity to the fore. Kenaan is critical of the presuppositions of the visual in Levinas' (and much of Western philosophical) thought, which is two-dimensional or, in a word, 'flat'. Harkening back to the dimensionality of culture, he brings to the fore the active dimensions of seeing, what, if we could use Kierkegaard's reflection from *Works of Love*, raises the question of seeing what one sees. This active understanding of seeing brings problems of agency to the fore and, consequently, the question of ethics at the heart of seeing. But since seeing transcends the two-dimensional, then the incompleteness and selection at work in acts of visualization raise the penumbral, the erasing, the determining, the distinguishing, the judging, and the many instances of actions beyond models premised upon identification and objectification, of intentional practices of adumbrating notions of 'there' and 'that'. This is groundbreaking stuff, reminiscent of the debate Edith Stein had with Husserl, where she identified an ethical dimension of phenomenological movements of reduction. It is a must-read for anyone seriously interested not only in visuality but also in the very condition of what it means to speak with responsibility about appearance.'

Lewis R. Gordon, Professor of Philosophy, African American Studies and Judaic Studies at the University of Connecticut at Storrs, and author of *Disciplinary Decadence*

The Ethics of Visuality

Levinas and the Contemporary Gaze

Hagi Kenaan

Translated by Batya Stein

I.B. TAURIS

LONDON · NEW YORK

The book was translated with the support of the Israel Science Foundation.

Published in 2013 by I.B.Tauris & Co. Ltd
6 Salem Road, London W2 4BU
175 Fifth Avenue, New York NY 10010
www.ibtauris.com

Distributed in the United States and Canada Exclusively by Palgrave Macmillan
175 Fifth Avenue, New York NY 10010

International Library of Contemporary Philosophy 3

ISBN: 978 1 78076 515 0 (HB)
         978 1 78076 516 7 (PB)

A full CIP record for this book is available from the British Library
A full CIP record is available from the Library of Congress

Library of Congress Catalog Card Number: available

Printed and bound in Great Britain by T.J. International, Padstow, Cornwall

Beyond the last image and before the first word
– facetalk

Contents

Acknowledgements

The Ethics of Visuality is a philosophical response to the gradual disappearance of the human face from the life-world of contemporary culture. The book was originally published in Israel, in Hebrew, within a society and a politics whose overall indifference to the address of the face has become unbearable. The book is dedicated to friends who refuse to live in a faceless world.

I thank Batya Stein for her careful translation and Liza Thompson for her unique way of welcoming the book.

Preface
The Rule of the Frontal

A: Where are you?
B: I'm in a traffic jam on the A4.

A cellular answer to a cellular question. This is state-of-the-art technology, and a new generation of phones is already available. Between the poles, however, another event has also taken place, one that the digital media cannot encode: you addressed me. A question was asked, and the question, though no more than yet another horizontal move in the boundless field of digital information, continued to resonate like a voice within a well. This resonance stems from the fact this digital question has a latent, albeit forgotten depth structure. In the current 'where are you?' question, an ancient one vibrates; 'new meat is eaten with old forks,' as Brecht writes. This ancient question is the one that opens, for example, the dialogue between Socrates and Phaedrus when there too, as on the highway, the question does not appear at the centre but indeed on the city's limit: 'Phaedrus, whence come you, and whither are you going?'[1] What are the coordinates between which you move? Where in between them are you located? What is your place? Originally, though, the question is even older – a divine question, the first question – the one addressed to Adam in the wake of the first sin: 'And the Lord God called to the man, and said to him, where are you?' (Genesis 3:9).

The 'where are you' question calls forth a kind of gaze that was new to humans. To situate himself, Man (Adam) was required to dislodge his gaze from its immersion in things seen 'there' and gather it back onto himself and onto the context in which his life unfolds. In order to answer the 'where' question, Adam is required

ix

to find a new viewpoint, external to the immediate flow of his experience; a viewpoint that only becomes accessible after having eaten from the tree of knowledge: 'And the eyes of them both were opened, and they knew that they were naked.' Eating from the tree of knowledge signals a threshold. Crossing this threshold makes them human.

By eating from the tree, Adam and Eve sin and are harshly punished even though they have not yet been initiated into the moral domain (the only domain wherein such punishment would be justified). They are punished whilst still lacking the ability to discern between good and evil. This ability will be granted to them only *ex post factum* and, in this sense, the first sin could not yet be ascribed to a moral subject. Indeed, not committed by a moral agent, the first sin is precisely what turned humans into ethical subjects. The ethical subject was born in sin, and not by chance: the only possibility of establishing the domain of human life as an ethical domain was contingent upon eating from the tree of knowledge, upon doing what retrospectively emerges as evil. Hence, by eating from the tree of knowledge, humans find themselves for the first time between poles in whose regard the question of orientation opens up, the question of how to locate oneself – the 'where are you?' question.

This radical transformation plays a constitutive role in the creation of the visual realm. Adam and Eve had been part of the visual from the start, but after eating from the tree of knowledge, a revolutionary change takes place: their eyes are opened. This change is indeed related to a reflective dimension that is added to the gaze and that had not been there before. But even before this reflexivity, there is something without which the gaze could not have returned to the one doing the looking. Underlying reflection is a visual vector that is created with the eating of the fruit and now becomes central. The essence of the gaze prior to the sin lies in an outward flow toward what is visually 'there,' presenting itself to the gaze, beyond the gazing, and embodied in a hand stretched out to grasp the fruit. By contrast, with the eating of the forbidden fruit, the gaze incorporates an opposite movement, which opens it up. This movement, coming from the outside, generates the possibility of vision through a disturbance it creates in penetrating the contracting core of the gaze, when it sears the optical nerve. One of the most familiar manifestations of this movement is the experience of shame.

The background for understanding the emergence of the reflective gaze is that, after eating from the tree of knowledge, good and evil have turned into the essential poles, the actual coordinates of the visual field. Henceforth, the visual field can no longer be understood as a neutral, transparent, formal domain that simply contains the totality of what encounters the eye. The visual is rather a realm constituted by strong directionality. It is a domain wherein one's location is always already meaningful in some specific way, a realm where one can find and lose, be close, closer, far, infinitely far. That is, the visual is a space of appearance wherein the question of orientation, the 'whither?' or 'where are you?' questions are, invariably, already an essential part of what appears.

Still, in order to allow the visual field to genuinely open up as an ethical domain, the 'where are you?' question cannot remain virtual but requires, in order to become actual, the conditions of 'orientation' and 'distantiality.' Distantiality is the very possibility of a movement constitutive of both proximity and distance: the possibility of opening up or closing distances, of altering an existing distance, of relocating vis-à-vis objects, the Other, or oneself: falling deep and rising high; turning one's back, being estranged; in exile; beyond the sea; crossing the sea; returning home; being at home, stepping into the yard; the street; becoming a stranger within the familiar. This possibility, which has no place in a space founded on fixed and fully determined distances, is elusive. Is distantiality present in the contemporary field of the image?

Considering contemporary visuality, the answer is far from obvious. When we specifically return to the traffic jam on the highway, it seems unclear how to begin answering the 'where?' question that was asked, even at the simple literal level. Where are you actually when you are in a traffic jam on the A4? What kind of place is a traffic jam on the highway? Does it not resemble more a non-place than a place with a specific identity? Neither a centre nor clear horizons, blinking lights, a multitude of other people in other cars, text messages, news flashes, threats of a nuclear disaster (a pundit), a man and a woman modelling leather pants, exorbitant giant billboards next to offhand graffiti, everything fragmentary, unruly, endless possibilities, parallel channels, intersecting channels, expanses of floating chatter crisscrossing time and again and creating endless 'media events,' adverts, all the time and everywhere – lots of noise and no attention. What, in this context, must we or can we pay attention to? And the eye too, or above all the eye, plunged into the constant flickering of images, large and small screens, at every angle, at every moment, in every possible size, always in plural. Where should it turn to?'

The current space of sense has been freed from the hegemony of questions, meanings and structures that had played such a crucial role in modernism: depth, perspective, history, hierarchy, the limits of the phenomenal, or the insoluble tension between the overt and the concealed. As such, the current space of sense may be viewed as a realization of a postmodern vision. The postmodern agenda was, in this sense, realized without leaving a remnant, without memory, that is, while eliminating its own critical potential as well as an entire horizon of alternatives, of crossroads where choices had still been possible. Modernist questions hardly resonate today, and neither do radical forms of opposition to these questions that had still been committed to confront – Foucault, Kristeva and Derrida – even if by negation, a system of basic distinctions including that between vision and representation, between representation and power, between the visual and the conceptual-linguistic, between the image and the real. To one engulfed in the beat of the current visual situation, these distinctions may now appear as useless wrecks, not only detached from their underpinnings in reality but also leaving an unclear sense as to the reality they ever spoke of.

As Baudrillard shows in regard to a phenomenon as ordinary as television, for example, neither Sartre's notion of the 'gaze'

– the gaze as a power in the frontal struggle for the right to be
– nor Foucault's subjectless model, the transparent rule of the
panopticon, can any longer be relevant: 'The eye of TV is no longer
the source of an absolute gaze, and the ideal of control is no longer
that of transparency.' In the current domain of meaning, of which
television is only one symptom,

> it becomes impossible to locate one instance of the model, of
> power, of the gaze, of the medium itself ... No more subject,
> no more focal point, no more center or periphery ... No
> more violence or surveillance: only 'information,'... chain
> reaction, slow implosion and simulacra of places in which the
> effect of the real again comes into play.[2]

But whereas Baudrillard could have declared in the 1980s that as 'we
are witnessing the end of perspectival and panoptic space ...' we are
facing 'the *very abolition of the spectacular*,'[3] today we seem to lack
even the possibility of making such a statement. The perspective from
which such a limit could have appeared, the perspective allowing
us to identify a certain 'end,' has ceased to exist altogether. In the
contemporary domain of sense, 'no's are no longer in existence;
there are no barriers in the formation of meaning. Everything
(simply) shows itself, everything is legible, which means everything
is marketable, speedy, streamlined; and because we can see and say
everything, we are no longer witnesses to anything.

Looking back at the incisive – far *too* incisive – analyses of
Baudrillard (or, in another way, of Virilio or Jameson), these
critiques were hard to digest in the 1980s. This is because
looking at the present straight in the eye is so hard, and all the
more so because they touched the painful spot of a deep loss.
Today, however, one no longer needs exceptional critical insight
– or actually no critical insight or indeed any insight at all – to
acknowledge the disappearance of meaning from the realm of mass
information and media, or to acknowledge the subjugation of the
entire realm of sense to what Fredrick Jameson calls the 'logic of

late capitalism.' The reason is that everything, including criticism, including the seeing of what is hidden, have become symptoms of what Baudrillard understands as a new order of nihilism, one which is 'more radical, more crucial than in its prior and historical forms' because it is 'indissolubly that of the system, and that of all the theory that still pretends to analyze it.'[4]

Not So Long Ago

Something has happened to our gaze. The experience of seeing has changed. The visual field has undergone a radical transformation. Images are certainly sharper than ever. Pixel resolution is constantly on the rise, but this sharpness only hides the fact that the sense of sight no longer senses, that the eye has arrived at a state of clinical death. The eye has not closed; indeed, it has actually gaped open in a manner that precludes its reopening. The contemporary eye has access to limitless visual information. It has no sense of the forbidden or of that not intended for seeing. The eye absorbs and frames absolutely everything: from police brutality to the new products that appear on the shelf. Everything in principle belongs to it. The eye can draw close to the grounds of Mars, see the Earth as it looks from a distance, wander between infinitely small particles of matter, plunge into the depths of the ocean, the bowels of the earth, or peek at the innermost organs of the human body, those that are called 'inner' because they were not necessarily meant for the eye.

The eye has become all-seeing, but this should be understood in the context of its subjugation to an inflation of blinking images that act upon it at every moment, from every direction. The eye has become a subject of the visual, a screen upon which changing contents ceaselessly appear: commercials and news. The eye has become used to surfing, naturally or seemingly naturally, over sequences lacking any centre or hierarchy that make room for, at varying levels of fusion and hybridity, the close and the far, the large and the microscopic, the old and the new, the original and the digitally reproduced, the real and the virtual.

The eye seems to have become used to tolerate everything. In the current political-technological-economic field, the eye is subject to a constant manipulation that not only blunts and depresses its sensitivity to important dimensions of the visual but, moreover, erases any remnant of an option to refuse the market rules operating upon it. Thus, for instance, though the level of horror and violence presented on various screens has gone up considerably in recent decades, nothing can truly shake the eye. The eye is flooded with images, swamped yet driven by a chronic hunger – rather than a desire – that does not seek meaning in the visual, only stimulation. In the age of digital image and high-speed communication, nothing the eye ever sees causes it to close up or retreat, because it has itself become addicted to stimulation. Stimulation has become its measure and, as such, nothing could ever truly excite it.[5] And more specifically for my purpose, an eye that swallows – or is swallowed – is a placeless eye. Severed from the 'where?' question, it is an eye whose space of experience eliminates the option of distantiality and, therefore, is estranged from the ethical dimension of the visual.

Hence, for example, as it turns itself toward the image that appears on the television screen, the computer screen, or the giant billboard, the eye knows only one form of relationship: an unchanging uniform distance. This is the case even though, in the narrow sense, a distance-nearness spectrum can be technically detected here as well, such as the zoom-in and zoom-out option that has become an integral part of our viewing routines. Indeed, the screen may open up the option of seeing in 'reduced' or 'augmented' size for us, but changing the scale – or changing our physical location vis-à-vis a screen – is merely a secondary addition to the uniformity of the distance dictated by the screen. In front of the screen and the information encoded in it, the living space of the eye yields to the domination of the homogeneous where all points of view take on identical form. Since the screen functions as a frame for contents packaged and served in a way that fits the consumer's needs to begin with, the manner of accessing the phenomenal, the angle of observation, the kind of involvement – the orientation, the self-positioning – do not play any actual role but constitute a minor and negligible by-product of what appears in front of us. And indeed, everything is already there, framed and frontally presented, for everyone and no one in particular. The various contents that appear on the screen always have an identical, essentially flat structure, not because of the screen's physical characteristics but rather because of the way in which the screen creates what Baudrillard calls the 'degree zero of meaning,' that is, a meaning whose internal form and constitutive logic is that of a commercial. Baudrillard writes:

> Today what we are experiencing is the absorption of all virtual modes of expression into that of advertising. All original cultural forms, all determined languages are absorbed in advertising because it has no depth, it is instantaneous and instantaneously forgotten. Triumph of superficial form ... The lowest form of energy of the sign ... All current forms of activity tend toward advertising and most exhaust themselves therein. Not necessarily advertising itself, the kind that is produced as such – but the *form* of advertising, that of a simplified operational mode, vaguely seductive, vaguely consensual ... in which all particular contents are annulled.[6]

To preserve its homogeneous format, the screen levels the visual to the lowest possible common denominator; the screen is 'levelled visuality,' the reduction of the visual to the frontal. The screen is the uttermost manifestation of the frontal. What appears on the screen already takes the gaze into account in a manner that is uniformly accessible: its visuality corresponds to only one perspective – one without texture, no dimensions of contact, no back or side, without shaded areas, cracks, tears – without hiding. Everything on the screen is always completely available and equally oriented outward toward the eye. But, this availability to sight does not mean sincerity or self-exposure but rather the erasure of the very distinction between inside and outside, between overt and concealed, between levels of reality. On the screen, the depth dimension of the visual, the time of the visual, the invisible or the visual's Other, are annulled. The screen is the contents it presents, in a synthetic present that neither grows from a specific past nor leads to a specific future. Beyond these contents there is nothing. The screen does not exist beyond then and, therefore, its sole concern is to capture the eye in a way that conceals the material substratum, the body of the appearances' surface. The screen is an entity whose *telos* is its own disappearance, and, in this sense, the impressive thinness that technology has succeeded in granting it is indeed an advanced stage in the realization of its essence as infinitely thin. As such, the screen is a typical example of the dual relationship that Baudrillard describes between the medium and its contents. On the one hand, 'all contents of meaning are absorbed in the only dominant form of the medium,' and on the other, 'the implosion of contents ... the absorption of meaning' is concomitant with the disappearance or 'evanescence of the medium itself.'[7]

Metonymically, the screen may henceforth be a helpful image when talking about a visual domain that has become flat and frontal (without thereby saying that everything that appears on screens is necessarily flat). The modus operandi of the frontal is perhaps binary, but its effect is total: what you see is what you get, and nothing else beside it. The screen shows all and everything can show itself on it, concealing the possibility of pointing to, of looking beyond, of transcending and, furthermore, of erasing any temptation or fantasy of doing so. The screen is what appears in front of us, and will always remain framed as frontal since its very design is intended for the eye – it controls the eye through absolute adaptation to its needs and, in particular, to its need to control the visual. The frontal is a visuality flattened to the measure of the eye; it is the structure of a horizonless phenomenon, detached from the horizontal dimension of our existence – the line uniting earth and sky – a structure that does not allow the gaze to move toward what will always remain beyond the visual.

The frontal domain has no outside and, therefore, no course that is ever internal: it has no path for drawing close to the visual from within. The screen is the absolutely accessible, but at the same time it does permit the eye to develop any visual closeness to it; it permits no encounter. And yet, as noted, what precludes such closeness is not an unbridgeable distance but the absolute erasure of the distance dimension, the elimination of the distinction between far and near; to put this differently, no relation of proximity to the screen is possible because the screen leaves nothing to draw close to. The screen will thus serve here as a metaphor for the pathology of contemporary visuality, for the homogeneity that the current condition imposes on the eye while making the eye forget its own inherent resources: its freedom and concomitant responsibility, its ability to be involved, its constant involvement, its ability to be critical, to be intimate, to sense shame, to refuse. Not to mention the possibility of not looking, of looking back, of looking beyond, of looking – like Thales, the first philosopher – upward, downward, obliquely, or of insisting on looking at what, at least at the beginning and perhaps also at the end, remains invisible.

The present work seeks to articulate an alternative to the rule of the frontal over the gaze, while recognizing that the frontal structure of the visual is not merely an artificial coating that can easily be jettisoned. The fact that our ordinary spaces of existence, both private and public, fill up with screens, only attests to the grip of the screen structure on our subjectivity. The screen today is not only one of the many options of visuality; rather, it makes a total demand, originating in the fact that our openness to the realm of sense is held captive by the frontal. We have lost the capacity to see the extent to which our existence has become screen-compatible, or more bluntly, after Baudrillard, that we ourselves have become the screen. Indeed, Baudrillard writes: 'There is no more hope for meaning. And without a doubt this is a good thing: meaning is mortal.'[8] The question of meaning may well disappear one day from human life. But so far, the concern with meaning is still so important and fundamental to our lives that I can hardly imagine humanity without this dimension. Thus, however troubling the frontal homogenization of sense may be, we must be wary of accepting and internalizing it as absolute, thereby crowning the frontal as a necessary and unchangeable condition, as an epitaph. We should free ourselves from the temptation to totalize the effect of our critical insights and prevent them from becoming yet another and perhaps more dire form of mental captivity. This often happens, for example, in the context of Baudrillard, when an essentially important and critical picture is used in the wrong dose.

The rule of the screen is indeed increasingly becoming entrenched as the basic structure of the appearance of meaning, and one of the prominent expressions of this entrenchment is the process of its becoming transparent. This totalitarian structure, however, is not as total as it presents itself to thought or to imagination. When a correct perspective is found – not at all a trivial task – the concrete appearance of the frontal, of the flat, reveals cracks and loopholes exposing many disruptions and breaches in the sequence. Though they usually remain hidden – despite, and perhaps because, they are in front of the eye – concrete acquaintance with them is a necessary condition for reopening the question of our orientation within the visual. But, what is there to be seen through these cracks?

The direction suggested in this work is not necessarily about seeing something *other* but rather learning to see *otherwise*. The kind of optics presented here as an alternative to the frontal, is one that begins with the refusal to accept the frontal as the standard of vision. This is a way of seeing that resists the fundamental condition of the screen: it cannot be framed because it is sensitive to a dimension of alterity that never converges into the cohesive structure of the packaged 'something' presented to the eye. This alterity is not abstract, and its concreteness constantly disrupts the frontal habits of the gaze. This is the seeing of the Other – not a seeing of *what* the case is, but of who is facing us – seeing her, seeing him, seeing you.

The possibility of seeing otherwise will be presented here through a discussion of the philosophy of Emmanuel Levinas who, in my view, opens up an unusual direction for grappling with the ethical dimension of the visual. Dealing with Levinas in this context may seem surprising at first glance, because Levinas shows no real interest in the visual, certainly no interest per se. Levinas does originate from a phenomenological tradition where the visual assumes a central role, but he himself has remained not only indifferent to the richness and hidden depths of the visual, but has also conveyed a kind of hostility, suspicion, or at least a profound ambivalence concerning the realm that appears to the eye. Levinas, who is known above all for the ethical turn he brings to philosophy, is troubled by what he understands as the fixated and fixating structure of the human gaze. For him, the visual is essentially a domain of levelled positive meanings, one that does not allow the ethical question to resonate as a primary question.

Despite his explicit stance, however, Levinas identifies at the core of the visual a site that is for him altogether exceptional: the scene of an extraordinary event that disrupts and unravels the fabric of what appears to the eye. This site is the human face or, more precisely, the face of the other person. The presence of the face creates a crack or a breach in the frontal order of the things that appear. 'The appearance in being of these "ethical peculiarities" – the humanity of man – is a rupture of being.'[9] This breach is, according to Levinas, the source of an alternative order (or actually a disorder): the revelation of the ethical. Thus, although the face is only an exception within the visual, its very existence requires, as I will show, a transformation in our understanding of the visual realm as a whole. The face that, according to Levinas, intersects the other person's speaking, epitomizes the human confrontation with a completely external question, a question that calls for, that demands, our response. For Levinas, as in the situation of the primordial 'where are you?' question, the life of the self unfolds constantly vis-à-vis a call whose source it cannot locate within the borders or the horizons of its grasp. The character of this call – appearing, according to Levinas, as a trace in the face as well as in the language of the other person – is the central theme of the present work.

The starting point of this work is an enigmatic statement that recurs in the writing of Emmanuel Levinas: 'ethics is an optics.' This saying, which requires a detailed explanation, creates a significant connection between the ethical and the optical. It calls us to think about the ethical in terms taken from visual theory: what is the connection between the question of moral obligation on the one hand, and the concern with the nature of light and the enabling conditions of the visual on the other? In what way can the visual frame the ethical question? In Levinas' writing, these questions are not addressed directly. To begin answering them, I shall first locate these questions in the context of the general philosophical move that preoccupies Levinas.

Ethics is an Optics
Preliminary Remarks

Emmanuel Levinas is a philosopher known above all for his ethics or, more precisely, for the ethical shift that he seeks to bring about in philosophy. Levinas' ethics is based on a unique understanding of the concept of the 'Other,' on the recognition of a radical alterity toward which systematic-conceptual thought has remained closed and blind. According to Levinas, this closure of Western thought reproduces a central tendency in our daily life: the tendency to forget, to ignore, to turn one's back on the demand of an alterity constantly present in our lives: the alterity of the other person. And yet, the ascription of an 'ethical shift' to Levinas does not refer only to the special place that the Other occupies in his ethics but, above all, to Levinas' very claim that ethics is 'First Philosophy.'

When Levinas claims that ethics is 'First Philosophy,' he challenges a deeply rooted – even if at times inconspicuous – order of priorities that characterizes Western philosophical tradition. This order of priorities precedes any specific philosophical discussion and finds expression, inter alia, in the privilege granted to the ontological question, the question of Being. By pointing to the primacy of ethics, Levinas seeks to undermine the tradition's accepted understanding that ontology comprises the most basic domain of philosophical questions, that is, the domain of questions addressing the being of things typically in terms of their essence. When the primary goal of thought is to obtain knowledge about the essence and being of things, the ethical question 'What

1

do I owe the other person?' necessarily takes second place. The ethical question does not disappear, but its radicalism is lost in a philosophical framework that internalizes ontology or epistemology as its foundation. According to Levinas, so long as we go on asking the question about our commitment to the other person in a way that depends on our ability to provide an exhaustive account of the other's essence, the ethical question cannot open up to the full. Rather, it functions as a convenient – all too convenient – question for thought, which poses no challenge and bears no trace of the unbridgeable distance between self and Other.

Self and Other

Levinas' ethics is based on a concept of alterity or, more precisely, on the recognition of an alterity that cannot be conceptualized. This alterity, according to Levinas, is what usually eludes the philosophical thought evolving under the hegemony of what he calls 'the same' (*le Même*): 'In it is dissolved the other's *alterity*.'[1] 'Western philosophy,' Levinas writes,

> has most often been an ontology: a reduction of the other to the same by interposition of a middle and neutral term that ensures the comprehension of being. The primacy of the same was Socrates' teaching: to receive nothing of the Other but what is in me.[2]

But the widespread tendency in the history of philosophy 'reducing to the same all that is opposed to it as *other*'[3] is not only a philosophical symptom. The hegemony of 'the same' in human thought, 'does not represent some abstract schema; it is man's ego.'[4] The philosophy of the same grows naturally from the ordinary and originates, more specifically, in patterns through which we live and organize our conception of selfhood.

The structure of the 'I,' according to Levinas, is neither simply given (as a something) nor is it a simple given (a datum). The 'I' on which our life pivots expresses a basic existential need for a form of life based on one unified, self-identical centre. The self, rather than present at birth, emerges through a gradual and constant process of self-constitution and self-maintenance that produce unity and identity. 'The existence of an ego takes place as an identification of the diverse. So many events happen to it, so many years age it, and yet the ego remains the same!'[5] In different texts, Levinas points to the various mechanisms that enable the self to create and preserve what seems to be the characteristic of selfhood familiar to us from the day-to-day. These mechanisms include, for example, our narrative power, which enables the integration of a multiplicity of events into one unified sequence; the ability to suspend the burden of the world; the ability to create, parallel to our existence among things, also the possibility of recoil – the discovery or invention of inwardness; the possibility of shaping the encounter with the world as part of the domestic and the familiar and, furthermore, the possibility of turning reality, turning the life we live into 'ours' through work and ownership.[6]

The fact that we succeed in endowing the 'I' with the structure of a unified self is, according to Levinas, an achievement that is far from being trivial. In his early writing, Levinas devotes extensive discussion to the manner in which the comprehensible appearance of reality is dependent on the constitution of the ego. Even the most minimal and basic appearance of sense in the form of a mere 'something' would not have been possible without the grounding of experience in a unified pole of self-identity. Without this structural stability, our field of experience would collapse and the ego would lose its ability to experience the world meaningfully.

And yet, notwithstanding the importance of assimilating and homogenizing mechanisms that enable the ego to stabilize within a space of meaning, the workings of these mechanisms also involve problematic implications. They exact a price: the internalization of the same as the stability principle of the 'I.' The establishment of the ego is, according to Levinas, 'the original event of the identification of the same.'[7] Furthermore, 'the I's identification, its marvellous autarchy, is the natural crucible of this transmutation of the other into the same.'[8] That is, the creation of the 'I' occurs together with the reduction of the Other.

Levinas' ethics grows out of a critique targeting a philosophical tradition that, in his view, consecrates the ego as its starting point. Levinas argues that Western philosophy, rather than criticizing the banal patterns that characterize the institution of the ego, embraces and internalizes selfhood as a guiding ideal. Philosophy, and particularly modern philosophy, surrenders to the 'plot' of the self to the point that the story of the 'I' becomes the narrative of philosophical thought. 'Philosophy is egology,'[9] Levinas writes – the logos of Western thought is the logos of the ego. The 'I' has become far more than a central theme in philosophical tradition. It functions (again, not always openly) as the structure (of identity, unity, and totality) that determines the horizons of thought as, to begin with, closed. Closed to what? To the troubling presence of a radical alterity that cannot be assimilated, brought home, or interpreted within the order of the same. In this sense, Levinas sees the philosophical alternative that he offers as the realization of a critical ideal whose 'critical intention … leads it beyond theory and ontology':

> Critique does not reduce the other to the same as does ontology, but calls into question the exercise of the same. A calling into question of the same – which cannot occur within the egoist spontaneity of the same, is brought about by the other. We name this calling into question of my spontaneity by the presence of the Other, ethics.[10]

Levinas seeks a course that will enable thought to be open to the presence of the Other while challenging the rule of the same. This challenge, Levinas emphasizes, cannot be posed out of what he calls 'egoist spontaneity,' a phrase that should be understood literally. 'Egoist spontaneity' is the spontaneity of the ego, that is, the sequence of immediate experience that provides and constantly confirms our sense of the ego. Egoist spontaneity is a platform for the workings of the philosophy of the same, and thus the antithesis of the possibility of critique. In the framework of a thought that belongs to the 'natural' and continuous flow of the ego, the hegemony of the ego cannot be called into question. The alterity of the Other could never become apparent to us from within ourselves. As the above passage shows, the possibility of the other's advent is related, rather, to a rupture occurring in the closed structure of the ego, to a disturbance that no longer allows the ego to go on assuming itself as obvious and self-evident. But this disruption is not something that takes place within the 'I.' Its origin lies outside. Subverting the rule of the same is not the result of an inner process of inference and understanding, but is 'brought about by the other.' A philosophy that does not fear being vulnerable and that allows itself to be shaken by the outside, ruptured by the presence of the Other, is what Levinas terms 'ethics.'[11]

Quite a broad spectrum of questions opens up at this stage. These questions are important for an understanding of Levinas, who answers some of them explicitly, some indirectly or incompletely, and some not at all. First, in what way precisely does philosophical thought impose the same on the Other? Is the history of philosophy homogeneous in its attitude to the Other, or does it also include unique moments wherein thought transcends the rule of the same? Does all conceptual thinking (is there a thinking that is non-conceptual?) necessarily dispel the Other's alterity? Is the levelling of the Other the 'built-in flaw' of Western philosophy? Is philosophical thought, by its very nature, essentially closed to the possibility of ethics? Accordingly, how should we understand the philosophy of Levinas himself? Does it not fall under the rubric of 'conceptual thinking'? And if not, is ethics as Levinas understands it altogether a philosophical possibility?

Beyond this, what is the significance of the Other's alterity that Levinas speaks of? In what sense can one ascribe to a person's alterity a meaning that transcends every conceptual system? Are you, for example, an Other in any sense, beyond the fact that you are you and I am I, beyond the fact that you were born in one place and I in another, that your biography differs from mine, that you chose a profession or a path different from mine, that you look different, that your gender is different from mine, that you know how to do things that I do not, that you have feelings that do not always concur with mine, and so forth? Is the Other's alterity – for instance your alterity – unintelligible, incomprehensible, so foreign to the context of our language and thought? Or perhaps quite the opposite: perhaps it is only because of our ability to make conceptual distinctions that we can altogether identify and distinguish ourselves from one another, see the difference – at times abysmal – between us?

In a slightly different formulation: is not the Other's alterity ultimately a function of a fundamental sameness, does it not necessarily assume a shared foundation? Levinas definitely tries to contend with such questions, and some of his answers will be relevant below. At this stage, however, note that even if we agree that some incomprehensible dimension is invariably present in the Other – something that will always elude us – the question still remains: in what way is this dimension at all fundamental to the ethical discussion, in what way does it contribute to an understanding of the essence of our obligations toward the Other? Or, more incisively, can radical alterity – one that is not part of our realm of meaning and understanding – serve at all as a basis for ethics? Is it possible for an ethical discussion to have no grounding in a domain of shared meaning? Should it not grow from the very comprehensibility of interpersonal space? Should it not take into account the general dimensions of the encounter with the Other that we not only can but are also required to understand (the value of human life, suffering, justice, rights), as well as the specific dimensions of an understanding of concrete distress in specific political and social contexts?

Writing and Desire

Levinas adopts a critical perspective regarding the philosophical in general. In his writing, he articulates a broad-ranging critique that hardly ever deals on the specific positions of particular thinkers (the source of both its strength and its weakness).[12] Levinas focuses on what he understands as the opening conditions of philosophical discourse, on the initial conceptual setting that, in his view, regulates and also encloses the space of Western thought. His critique is not preoccupied with the contents of any specific philosophical picture but offers instead a structural insight: there is something in the structure of thought, in the way that thought prepares itself for its journey, that closes fundamental horizons, locks paths and erases options, ultimately hiding truth from us.

In this sense, the history of philosophy is for him the history of a pathology. This rhetoric is not new for Levinas, who became acquainted with it through the teachers he adopted: Husserl, the philosophical father figure he chose for himself, and then, Heidegger. More generally, Levinas could be said to belong to a family of philosophers who understand themselves, their thought, and their philosophical innovation through opposition to the philosophical tradition to which they belong. Resembling philosophers such as Kierkegaard, Nietzsche, or even Wittgenstein (and unlike philosophers such as Kant, Hegel, or even Sartre), Levinas writes out of a deep ambivalence toward the philosophical canon, the setting for his growth and development.

Levinas writes in philosophical language. Philosophy is his language, it is the home, the place from which he looks at and thinks about the world. But this language is also what hinders, in his view, the possibility of opening up toward, being responsible for what ultimately is most important for him. The position he takes toward the philosophical tradition and its language is double-edged. Levinas writes with a sense of ambivalence: he is a scion of the tradition but also a foreigner, a '*xenos*' within it. In itself, this ambivalence is not specific to Levinas but is a sign that differentiates between two kinds of philosophical starting points. Levinas belongs with those philosophers whose starting point is complicated, preventing them from expressing their thought simply and directly. This, however, is not so much because the content of their thought is exceptionally complex but because they cannot find in the language they speak the possibility of expressing what they see or seek.

And yet – and this is perhaps the more surprising side – Levinas, again like Heidegger, does not view his critique and the radical alternative he proposes as a kind of departure from philosophy but, on the contrary, as a path that leads the tradition to realize its inner essence. He does identify in the tradition a serious pathology, and release from it necessitates a fundamental change in the life of the mind. But precisely through the liberation from patterns that seem essential to Western philosophical thought, in parting ways with the tradition, Levinas seeks to return metaphysics to its origins, to return to it a basic and precious dimension it has lost: its desire.

Something is slightly strange in this rhetoric, but possibly interesting as well. Levinas speaks of the distortion of the ethical essence in philosophical thought. Unlike Heidegger, who returns to the pre-Socratics, Levinas does not pine for some early era in the history of philosophy, when thought purportedly realized the openness and responsibility that he considers philosophy's aim. Levinas does indeed point to the existence of moments with ethical potential, moments that are flashes of light in the history of philosophy, such as Plato's claim about the presence of the good beyond being, or Descartes' formulation of the idea of infinity. Overall, however, he views Western philosophy as having remained far removed from its ethical origins, even though it had never truly been close to this source.

Levinas makes a point about losing, distorting, or drawing away from, a dimension fundamental to philosophy, although this dimension had never been appropriated nor truly owned by philosophy. Can we lose what we never had? Can the metaphysical desire of which Levinas speaks be considered essential to philosophy despite the fact that it had not been an integral part of its history? Scorsese's film *No Direction Home* opens with a monologue by Bob Dylan dealing with life as a search for a lost home. Dylan speaks of his life as an odyssey. Yet, whereas the purpose of Odysseus' voyages was to find a way back to his home in Ithaca, to his kingdom, to his wife and son who had been waiting for him for years, Dylan speaks of a return journey to a home he never had:

> Like an odyssey of going home somewhere, I set out to find this home that I'd left a while back … and I couldn't remember exactly where it was, but I was on my way there … I was born very far from where I was supposed to be. So, I'm on my way home, you know

The Ethical and the Optical

This work begins with Emmanuel Levinas' saying that 'ethics is an optics.' What is the connection between the ethical and the optical, between the question of moral obligation and the concern with the nature of light and the enabling conditions of the visual? In the context of Levinas' strongly transcendent position, whereby the origin of a moral imperative absolutely transcends what can appear to the eye, the answer to this question is far from obvious. Not only is Levinas' attempt to tie the transcendent to the realm of visuality unclear, but his very interest in the character of the visual space is incompatible with the hostility, or at least the suspicion, he displays toward the domain visible to the eye.

Levinas' critical statements about the fixated and fixating structure of the human gaze extend further, colouring with deep ambivalence his attitude toward the visual arts. In the course of time, Levinas has softened his position concerning art and made it more complex, but even in his later responses to art we can hardly fail to hear the echo of the biblical commandment 'Thou shalt not make unto thee any graven image.' This command presupposes, even before the prohibition itself, the need for clear separation between the divine and the secular that, by its very essence, is tied to what the eyes see.

To put this in other terms, what often resonates in Levinas' references to the visual arts is the Platonic warning against the autonomy of the image. The visual image is problematic not only because it fails to present the transcendent but also because it has the power to level and corrupt the value of the infinite. Surprisingly, however, the visual plays a central role in Levinas' writing, creating a conceptual tension that is at times troubling and not always soluble. One prominent example of the presence of such tension is Levinas' usage of the concept or image that constitutes the centre of this volume: the human face (*le visage*). According to Levinas, the face is testimony to the Other's absolute alterity, a transcendent alterity that establishes, beyond any perception, the moral imperative. As such, the face does not essentially belong to the visual. Indeed, Levinas claims that the face is not at all a visual phenomenon, a claim not easily reconcilable with its obvious visuality.

Levinas' use of the concept of the face, then, is antithetical, at least ostensibly, to our usual way of relating to human faces. Can we think or imagine a face lacking a visual appearance? Why does Levinas choose an image so typically visual in order to speak of what in principle cannot appear to the eye? Has Levinas made an unsuccessful choice here? What is the philosophical legitimacy of a conceptual use of this sort? Such questions recur often in the writing about Levinas and lead, on the one hand, to interpretations attempting to solve, temper, or conceal the salient tensions in his thought, and on the other, to critiques targeting the validity of his conception of the face.[13] But these two contrasting approaches hide, albeit in different ways, an important aspect of Levinas thought: the fact that the troublesome presence of internal tension is fundamental to Levinas' own project. The tension between the visual and the non-visual dimensions of the Other's face is not only a problem but also an expression of the Other's form of appearance, its mode of givenness. The Other is what is present and revealed, according to Levinas, through the tension between the visible and the invisible, the phenomenal and the transcendent, the conceptual and what cannot be conceptualized – a strong tension that is very hard to live with.

Levinas, then, is a philosopher of tensions. His writing is so prominently suffused with them that, ultimately, they preclude any possibility of his thoughts coalescing into a systematic philosophical method. Levinas' writing cannot 'uphold' a coherent structure to the end, but it does not attempt to do so either. The ideal of a philosophical method is not set up as a goal for Levinas and, moreover, it contradicts his understanding of the role and vocation of thought. Nevertheless, Levinas' critique of the philosophical yearning for totality does not, in itself, result in anarchy or lead to the fragmentary. Although the ineffable is a permanent horizon in Levinas' writing, the question of philosophical style is not explicitly related for him to the confrontation with the limits of language. Unlike a philosopher such as Kierkegaard, for example, Levinas does not deal explicitly with linguistic devices – such as the structure of paradox – that can help the author reconstruct the encounter, the friction effect, with the limit of words. The tensions resonating in Levinas are not a deliberate product of his writing. They are not methodological but rather the expression of a kind of sensitivity or attention to unsolved dimensions in the structure of the appearance of things themselves. In this sense, Levinas is fundamentally a phenomenologist, even if he wages a relentless struggle with phenomenology and, ultimately, indeed releases himself from it.

More specifically, resonating in Levinas' writing is an insoluble tension originating in the concrete presence of the transcendent within the ordinary, a trace that can be gleaned in the 'face' and 'speaking' of the Other. According to Levinas, the fact that the transcendent is unattainable or incapable of conceptualization does not imply that it is located far beyond the horizons of thought, so that we can altogether ignore it and live without it. Quite the contrary: the transcendent is revealed in the 'here and now' – the invisible shows itself as such. And yet, the transcendent is not what belongs, as in Merleau-Ponty, for example, to the inner – even if concealed – pulse of everydayness. The invisible does not hide between the lines, as raindrops that remain hanging on a treetop or as the depth of a pool seen through the water. Rather, for Levinas, the invisible is what disturbs the harmony of the visible. It ruptures the visible, thus creating a surprising effect, often troubling and difficult and at times painful and uncomfortable, like a smashed window, or the unfamiliar sound of steps in the house.

But before turning to a discussion of the human face and to the way it breaches the harmony of the visual, it is worth unravelling Levinas' saying that 'ethics is an optics' in terms slightly more precise. First, note that this phrase appears twice in the introduction to *Totality and Infinity*, in two different but analogous contexts. In both contexts, Levinas ties moral responsiveness to the possibility of an openness to what transcends the limits of experience. The statement that 'ethics is an optics' appears first at the end of a brief discussion opening the book on the nature of eschatological thought. Levinas writes:

> The eschatological vision breaks with the totality of wars and empires in which one does not speak. It does not envisage the end of history within being understood as a totality, but institutes a relation with the infinity of being which exceeds the totality. The first 'vision' of eschatology ... reveals the very possibility of eschatology, that is, the breach of the totality, the possibility of a *signification without a context*. The experience of morality does not proceed from this vision – it *consummates* this vision; ethics is an optics. But it is a 'vision' without image, bereft of the synoptic and totalizing objectifying virtues of vision, a relation of an intentionality of a wholly different type – which this work seeks to describe.[14]

Levinas' optical image appears against the backdrop of his attempt to locate the ethical beyond the political and the historical, in whose context we cannot understand what true peace is.[15] Peace, according to Levinas, is not a by-product of the political situation, which is essentially a situation of war. Nor is peace part of a historical sequence where, between wars, we can occasionally identify islands of tranquillity. To understand the possibility of peace out of and from within itself, utopian thought is required, a transcendent vision.

As an example of such a vision, Levinas makes a point of the manner in which eschatological thought relates to historical time. In its insistence on thinking about the end of time, eschatology is an instance of the human ability to think beyond history: it is an intentional stance relating to a time that will never be part of the totality of history. The movement of historical time turns all future into present and ultimately into past (and the past, accordingly, is what had once necessarily belonged to the future and then to the present). Messianic time, however, consists of a horizon of absolute future, a future that will always remain future, always exterior to the present, never belonging to the past. Eschatology is an example of a kind of thinking that acknowledges the existence of an irreducible, unbridgeable distance between itself and its object, a distance that, for Levinas, is fundamental to the understanding of the ethical relationship between the ego and the Other.

As in the eschatological perspective, then, Levinas offers an understanding of the ethical relationship based on a unique kind of vision. This vision is oriented, on the one hand, toward what appears to the eye, yet it also lacks all the characteristics that define the essence of visual perception. Not only is this kind of seeing non-perceptual but it is actually opposed to perception: in drawing close to what appears, this seeing finds in it the infinitely far. This, as noted, is 'a wholly different type' of intentionality, 'a vision without image.'

Thus when, slightly later in the book, Levinas returns to the optical image of ethics, he does so again in the context of a discussion about the philosophical need to recognize and describe a unique kind of intentionality that will be the cornerstone of his philosophical project:

If, as this book will show, ethical relations are to lead transcendence to its term, this is because the essential of ethics is in its *transcendent intention*, and because not every transcendent intention has the noesis-noema structure. Already of *itself* ethics is an 'optics.'[16]

The essence of the ethical is based, according to Levinas, on a unique form of intending the transcendent, an intentionality that contrasts with the Husserlian 'noesis-noema structure,' which had so influenced Levinas' early work.

Intentionality and the Idea of Infinity

Elucidating Husserl's philosophy in an early text, Levinas explains the term 'intentionality' as follows:

The characteristic that necessarily belongs to the whole sphere of consciousness ... is to be always 'consciousness of something.' Every perception is perception of the 'perceived'; every desire is desire of the 'desired,' etc. Husserl calls this fundamental property of consciousness intentionality.[17]

Intentionality refers to the structure of 'about-ness' constitutive of consciousness: the fact that consciousness is always directed at something (an object, a state of affairs), that it is always a bearer of content. At the same time, as Levinas himself often emphasizes, Husserl's concept of intentionality denotes not only some property or faculty but refers to a deep and essential dimension of consciousness, that is, to that structure that turns consciousness into what it is. Intentionality is consciousness' fundamental form of being. What makes the Husserlian position revolutionary, according to the early Levinas, is the understanding that consciousness itself is a *relation* and that, as such, it cannot be understood only in itself, independently of the world toward which it is always open:

It must be clearly understood that intentionality is not a bond ... between consciousness on one side and the real object on the other. Husserl's great originality is to see that the 'relation to the object' is not something inserted between consciousness and the object: it is consciousness itself. It is the relation to the object that is the primitive phenomenon – and not a subject and an object that would supposedly move toward one another.[18]

Consciousness is not an independent, closed and self-contained domain confronting the world; it is not a private field of subjective events or the inside of some black box or camera obscura containing only copies, representations, or reflections of the real things outside. Instead, the intentional structure should itself be understood as an opening: consciousness is the very opening of a world. Consequently, what is revealed to us in the field of experience is not an image or a representation of things and events belonging to the world, but the world itself. In his early writings, Levinas expresses his admiration for Husserl's innovation, and particularly for the open structure of a consciousness that always transcends itself, invariably affected by dimensions of sense that precede any specific content. And indeed, in the later context of *Totality and Infinity*, Levinas once again explicitly mentions his debt to Husserl:

The presentation and the development of the notions employed owe everything to the phenomenological method. Intentional analysis is the search for the concrete. Notions held under the direct gaze of the thought that defines them are, nevertheless, unbeknown to this naïve thought, revealed to be implanted in horizons unsuspected by this thought; these horizons endow them with a meaning – such is the essential teaching of Husserl. What does it matter if in the Husserlian phenomenology taken literally these unsuspected horizons are in their turn interpreted as thoughts aiming at objects. What counts is the idea of the overflowing of objectifying thought by a forgotten experience from which it lives.[19]

And yet, despite this clear acknowledgement, one can hardly ignore Levinas' critique of Husserl's concept of intentionality, a critique that only intensifies as Levinas emerges as an independent philosopher. Embracing the Husserlian openness of intentional consciousness to meaning-creating horizons that precede the familiar pattern of the object, Levinas nevertheless reads Husserl as missing the radical potential of his own discovery. Husserl, according to Levinas, ultimately restricts the notion of the intentional to an object-dependent relationship based on representation. Since the object, by definition, completely corresponds with the structure of consciousness, the common understanding of consciousness in terms of 'thoughts aiming at objects' prevents Husserl from developing the vision fundamental to ethical life.

Levinas understands the essence of the ethical in a manner that resists intentional analysis, at least in the Husserlian sense. He wishes to deconstruct the basic frame of correspondence between *noesis* and *noema*, between the specific intentional act (seeing, thinking, desiring, remembering, longing and so forth) and the intentional object, which always presents itself to consciousness according to the latter's measure (as the seen, thought, desired, remembered and so forth). The very attempt to part ways with the framework of intentionality is well known in the post-Husserl phenomenological tradition. Indeed, the significant developments in twentieth-century phenomenology all follow from a search for new areas of non-intentional experience. Thus, Levinas' attempt to gain release from the narrow signification of 'objecthood' is both natural and, in itself, not unique. His uniqueness in this context is the very specific direction he chooses in order to describe this non-intentional openness that, according to him, is so fundamental to ethics.

Before examining Levinas' alternative, however, it bears mention that his insistence on tying the ethical question to a question about the structure of experience (intentional or not) is far from obvious.

Can an exceptional case of meaningfulness serve as grounds for the ethical? How so? Is this not a conflation? Can ethical thought allow itself to be based only on one specific form of the subject's intentionality? Is it not required to serve in itself as a basis for a whole spectrum of forms of intuition? Can Levinas point to a privileged form of intentionality – one bearing an 'ethical' potential – without inevitably presupposing a given ethics as a basis? In other words: even if, following Levinas, we recognize the possibility of a non-intentional consciousness, how can we justify our acceptance of this non-standard as constitutive of the ethical?

For Levinas, the ethical question is indeed closely related to the question about the primary conditions wherein meaning appears. Contrary to Husserl, and influenced by Heidegger, Levinas refuses to accept a predominant philosophical picture that makes the subject's cognitive capability a constitutive condition of meaning. He refuses to locate the eventfulness of meaning in the epistemological and essentially neutral relationship between the subject and the world of objects. For him, the primary manifestation of meaning does not occur along the self-world axis or out of a subject-object relationship, but at a primordial and more profound level. The uncovering of this level is, for Levinas, crucial to the understanding of the conditions that enable the suchness of the world to appear.

Levinas, then, claims that the common tendency to relate to meaning as if it were a kind of object downplays more primary dimensions of the field of sense, dimensions that cannot find expression within the objective setting determined by cognitive consciousness. Furthermore, the object and its characteristics can appear before consciousness as meaningful only because consciousness is already open to a more basic layer of meaning. The world of sense can present itself to us through such discrete and familiar signification-forms as 'it's raining,' 'it's cold today,' 'the phone is ringing,' or 'there's a traffic jam' only because these options are found within a field where more primary vectors operate, allowing for the appearance of these specific entities and their characteristics.

Levinas finds inspiration for this mode of openness, which always precedes and underlies the relationship of consciousness with objects, in the Cartesian concept of 'the idea of infinity.' He states that 'Intentionality, where thought remains an *adequation* with the object, does not define consciousness at its fundamental level. All knowing qua intentionality already presupposes the idea of infinity, which is pre-eminently *non-adequation*.'[20]

In his use of the term 'idea of infinity,' Levinas returns to a philosophical moment he considers fundamental to the philosophy of Descartes, the father of modern philosophy. Descartes' concept of the *cogito* – the thinking self – is for Levinas a representative example of the philosophical 'egology' that essentially remains blind to the demand of the Other. And yet, he still finds in Descartes a different intuition that he identifies with, an intuition Descartes formulates in *Meditations* when dealing with the concept of God and, specifically, when considering one particular strand for the proof of God's existence.

For Descartes, the very presence of the concept of God within consciousness teaches us an important lesson. The concept of God brings consciousness face to face with a dimension that, prima facie, it cannot possibly contain: the infinite. How is the infinity of God present within us? First, as finite creatures with an essentially finite consciousness, what we can derive from within ourselves is a negative concept of infinity. The concept of the infinite is produced by the mind when it applies the negation operator to all that is finite and familiar to us. According to Descartes, however, this negative understanding proves insufficient for describing the original mode of God's presence in human consciousness. He holds that consciousness, despite its finitude, is open to the presence of the infinite in an immediate manner rather than only by way of negation. Surprisingly, then, our finite consciousness is characterized by its ability to also make room for an idea that resonates with God's infinite emanation. The idea of infinity is an opening to what transcends the limits of consciousness: it is a unique possibility of transcendence, one that flows from the immediate presence of infinity itself rather than from the limitations posed by the mind's finitude.[21]

The presence of the infinite in our finite consciousness leads Descartes to argue in favour of the existence of an infinite source external to humans – God – without which we could not explain the existence of the idea of the infinite within us. When Levinas considers Descartes' proof of the existence of God, he is not interested in the question of its validity but only takes from it the paradoxical image of a consciousness that thinks beyond what it can. The Cartesian conception of the idea of infinity recurs often in Levinas. Indeed, it becomes the key image through which he tends to mark the need to acknowledge the existence of a non-cognitive intentionality, an openness within us toward the dimension of transcendence, of distance, that can never be retracted:

> The alterity of the infinite is not cancelled, is not extinguished in the thought that thinks it is. In thinking infinity the I from the first *thinks more than it thinks.* Infinity does not enter into the idea of infinity, is not grasped; this idea is not a concept. The infinite is the radically, absolutely, other.[22]

Like Heidegger, Levinas also begins with a critique of how the *modus operandi* of representational thought conceals what thought cannot frame. Yet, whereas this critique takes Heidegger beyond beings to the question of Being, Levinas understands the shift to the question of Being as ultimately a recurrence of the flaws characterizing the thought of totality. Contrary to Heidegger, who turns to pure Being or to absolute nothingness, Levinas is wary of endorsing what appears to him as the diametrical opposite of Husserl's concept of intentionality. He seeks to avoid this type of negative picture because it leads, even if by contrast, to the same conceptual framework from which he seeks release. Instead, the alternative he offers is based on a 'transmutation' – or, in fact, 'a double transmutation' – of Husserl's intentionality. What opens up for him the basic possibility of sense is neither the relationship between a subject and objective content nor, as in Heidegger, the relationship between self and nothingness. Levinas points to a more primary vector, which connects the subject to an infinite alterity. Rather than abstract, however, this alterity is concrete and embodied in the relationship with the other person: 'Welcoming the Other ... in it, the idea of infinity is consummated.'[23]

In contrast to Descartes, then, for Levinas 'infinity is not the object of contemplation'[24] nor is it, in contrast to Heidegger, what awaits thought's uncovering or releasing. What concerns Levinas is an uncharted movement of transcendence that reveals itself to the self in the presence of the Other. The transcendent dimension of the Other is not only what escapes the ego's apprehension but also what compels it to contend with an external standard: 'in his face, the other appears to me not as an obstacle, not as a menace I evaluate, but as what measures me.'[25] The transcendent presence of the Other creates within the core of the ordinary an absolute and inaccessible measure for the self that is experienced as a permanent burden: a disruption of those ego mechanisms that enable consciousness to live as if it were the centre of the world.

> One must have the idea of infinity ... to know my own imperfection. The infinite does not stop me like a force blocking my force; it puts into question the naïve right of my powers, my glorious spontaneity as a living being ... the idea of infinity is the collapse of a quietism administered by the conscience of the same.[26]

The gaze that is born with this collapse, a collapse that is typically silent and microscopical, is precisely what concerns me in this work: what faces us when the rule of the object is undermined is not the Nothing but the Other.

Face

Face 1
The Gleam of Infinity

Levinas' most significant discussion on the question of the face is found in Part Three of *Totality and Infinity*, entitled 'Exteriority and the Face.' In this central work, as in his other texts, Levinas' concern with the face appears only in the 'second act,' that is, following a discussion and construction of a more general philosophical agenda. Rather than dealing with the face as an intriguing human phenomenon, Levinas sees it as attesting to the very possibility of the alternative starting point that his philosophy hinges upon. In *Totality and Infinity*, the question of the face surfaces already in the introduction when Levinas writes:

> We can proceed from the experience of totality back to a situation where totality breaks up, a situation that conditions the totality itself. Such a situation is the gleam of exteriority or of transcendence in the face of the Other.[1]

Although this initial mention is brief and concise, it does clarify the place of the face in Levinas' programme. The need to deal with the face emerges due to the deeply problematic way in which philosophical tradition presupposes its sphere of action and, specifically, to the widespread philosophical tendency to internalize an ideal of totality that gives thought confidence in its power to realize its freedom without any limits. The expression 'experience of totality' refers to thought as experiencing its (ostensibly) boundless movement, unfailingly succeeding in penetrating and

23

decoding the unknown, making the unintelligible intelligible and ultimately returning home.

The problem that Levinas points out, then, lies in the dominant tendency to build the field of philosophical thought and discourse as, in principle, an all-encompassing space capable of containing simply everything. In such a space, thought makes sense of everything that is foreign to it, explains it (endows it with meaning and gives it order), makes it familiar, attainable, subservient to the general picture or method. Yet, when philosophical tradition internalizes this ideal of 'totality' and allows it to control the life of thought, it pays a price. For Levinas, the price is the structural closure of philosophical discourse to what he calls 'infinity,' 'transcendence,' or 'Otherness.' This closure, although deeply entrenched in philosophical tradition, is not only unnecessary but actually derives, as evident from the passage cited above, from a prior position that is a condition of it. This primary condition is revealed with the collapse of the totality familiar to us, a totality that has the ego as its core and its principle of action. Levinas, then, points here to an alternative situation wherein we are no longer trapped in the 'spontaneity of the ego' but open beyond our own selves – beyond the scope of consciousness – to a strong alterity that confronts us even before we make room for it within ourselves. 'Such a situation,' he writes, 'is the gleam of exteriority or of transcendence in the face of the Other.'[2]

The desire for totality is the yearning to contain an uncontainable infinity. The name of the book, *Totality and Infinity*, conveys this fundamental tension between the structure of a yearning that sets the course of philosophical thought and the basic dimension of reality that remains, according to Levinas, foreign, transcendent and unreachable. In Western philosophical tradition, the urge for totality apparently succeeds in realizing itself by attaining infinity deceitfully, that is, in a way that assuages and neutralizes the living and disturbing presence of the infinite: the harsh demand that this presence imposes on us. Philosophy has many ways of killing the transcendent. It can obliterate the memory of the transcendent as, for instance, in various types of positivist thought. Yet, philosophy can also erase the infinite when honouring it, by turning it into an object of thought, a concept that can be grasped.

Levinas searches for a different kind of relationship with the infinite, and it is precisely at this point that the tie to the human face is established. At first glance, Levinas could have been understood as making a general claim about the need for acknowledging the importance of strong transcendence, given the erosion in its theoretical standing. Such claims are not unknown in the history of philosophy and, in this context, Levinas' uniqueness lies in the specific way in which he translates the general abstract claim about transcendence into the concrete and ordinary: Levinas calls attention to a presence of the infinite that cannot be integrated into a conceptual scheme. He is neither negating the concept of finitude nor offering a concept that is implied or can be inferred from an alternative conceptual system. The infinite, the transcendent, cannot be a concept in either sense, but it does not therefore follow that it is not present in our lives. Strong transcendence is the ground (perhaps the abyss) at the basis of our shared world, and this is not an abstract metaphysical insight but, according to Levinas, an insight originating in actual experience. Transcendence penetrates the most banal patterns of our life, breaking through the ego's personal and social forms of organization, through the landscapes of the same. When? How? In what way? According to Levinas, all the time: now, before dinner; facing a pizza delivery boy in the stairwell, a while ago; the look of a man on the other side of the pedestrian crossing or at the grocer's, running into a woman buying an ice cream for her daughter – we say hello or perhaps fail to do so. The gleam of transcendence appears 'in the face of the Other.'

Levinas, then, turns to the face to denote a kind of experience that fractures the totality ideal guiding Western philosophical thought. The face, in his view, concretely expresses the living presence of an infinite dimension that cannot be conveyed through a reflective language aspiring to totality. The face is a testimony. But what kind of testimony can a face provide? Does it indeed have a latent philosophical potential that enables an alternative beginning?

Several additional questions emerge here. First, if the transcendent is simply present in our day-to-day encounter with the face of the Other, why do we need philosophy in order to reveal it? If infinity (or alterity) is indeed such an integral part of our day-to-day life, why does it remain hidden? If all one needs to do to be persuaded of the transcendent is look the Other straight in the eye, why do we live our lives under the hegemony of the same? In what way is the transcendent present in the face? Is it openly there, like the graffiti on the wall of the corner bank? And if so, why is it still hidden from us? Does it perhaps hide like Peter Parker behind the Spider-Man mask? And if so is it at all correct to say that the transcendent is found in the face we see? Alternatively, if we say that the transcendent does not actually appear in the face as such, are we not falling back into the metaphorical use of the concept of 'face' and into an entirely abstract metaphysical claim about the transcendent?

Furthermore, we must ask whether and in what way the human face can jeopardize the hegemony of totality. Why altogether ascribe the power to evade the spheres of the ego to the face? Is it at all possible to speak about someone's face in a way that is not already the content of some consciousness looking, thinking, remembering? Is there, in this sense, an essential difference between the face's principle of appearance and the way objects generally appear before us – a leg, a hand, a table, a cup, an ashtray, a car on the road, shutters, a dog under the lamp post? Always in some particular consciousness, within a given set of coordinates, in a particular context or perspective?

Hence, is not the face as such always subject already to the rule of the same? Is not the appearance of the face necessarily part of the general and familiar frame of signification: big head or small head, spiritual face, sexy face, broad or narrow, wearing a skullcap, bald, hawk-nosed or pug-nosed, green eyes or blue eyes, Israeli, the face of a Jew, the face of a Palestinian, or, in more nuanced details, an English Jew (fourth generation), a Palestinian in Sweden, an German in Firenze (a tourist), a Turk in Germany, a Romanian (guest worker) in Tel Aviv, a witness to a terrorist attack, on TV, blood on the sleeve, a soldier, the Prime Minister of Lebanon crying, Tony Blair smiling, Nassaralla smiling, a young face, an adult face, an old face (in a bomb shelter, in nature, at the employment bureau, at a café), a child's face, a happy face, a yawn, anger, a contrite face, an arrogant face, self-confidence, scar-face, a face with a tic, a scream, someone singing. This is a broad spectrum of options, but all seemingly belong to a space of given meanings, which can be contextually verbalized, interpreted, and understood. Not so?

Levinas himself poses quite similar questions at the opening of Part Three of *Totality and Infinity*: 'Is not the face given to vision? How does the epiphany as a face determine a relationship different from that which characterizes all our sensible experience?'[3] The focal point here is the manner in which the appearance of the transcendent in the face bears on the relationship of the face to the visual: Can the phenomenality of the face accommodate transcendence? Can the transcendent ever be part of what we see, part of a structure of sensory perception with the ego at its core? And consequently, does the face belong to the visual? These questions require consideration of the face's unique form of appearance, something that can hardly be done apart from a broader discussion about the essence of appearance, of visuality, of being seen.

We have reached a crossroads here. Levinas' discussion of the transcendent as an alternative to totality – indeed, the basis of his ethics – intersects with a discussion from a seemingly different realm: visuality and the question of visual meaning. How should we understand this intersection? Historically, Levinas comes from a tradition wherein the concern with the question of appearance is central. Phenomenology aims to uncover the logos of the phenomenon and *Totality and Infinity* is clearly a phenomenological inquiry. Yet, the intersection between the questions here, between ethics and meaning, between alterity and visuality, is not simply a matter of a debt to, or a legacy from, the phenomenological tradition. This intersection is neither accidental nor generic but expresses instead the essence of Levinas' philosophical project. For Levinas, ethics is, above all, a theory of meaning. Ethics is an optics.

Face 2
How a Face Looks

The face of the Other is always there, as near as sweat to skin but also further than the moon. Although this tension between near and far, between visible and invisible, is fundamental to the appearance of the face, this duality is at times hard to uphold. It tends to clash with basic habits typical of our behaviour in the realm of the visual such as, for instance, our common tendency to internalize the television screen as representing the field of vision and, more generally, with entrenched intuitions concerning the relationship between surface and depth, appearance and essence, what is revealed and concealed from the eye. Levinas does not make our task any easier in this regard. On the one hand, he chooses the term 'face,' which calls forth a clear visual context, and on the other, he takes pains to emphasize repeatedly that, for him, the face does not belong to the visual. If what concerns Levinas is indeed a non-visual dimension of the Other's presence, why does he choose to identify this presence with the face?

In *Ethics and Infinity*, when Levinas is asked to clarify this tension, he draws a distinction between two ways of approaching the face: 'I wonder if one can speak of a look turned toward the face, for the look is knowledge, perception. I think rather that access to the face is straightaway ethical.'[1] For Levinas, the face is not what appears to the gaze. What is important in the face is precisely what is lost if one thinks of it as an object of vision:

You turn yourself toward the Other as toward an object when you see a nose, eyes, a forehead, a chin, and you can describe them. The best way of encountering the Other is not even to notice the color of his eyes! When one observes the color of the eyes one is not in social relationship with the Other. The relation with the face can surely be dominated by perception, but what is specifically the face is what cannot be reduced to that.[2]

The human gaze and vision in general are for him a clear exemplification of the intentional structure of consciousness. Levinas understands the act of vision (mistakenly, in my view) as a kind of cognitive representation that, by its very essence, is closed off to the infinite: 'Vision is not a transcendence ... It opens nothing that, beyond the same, would be absolutely other.'[3]

The gaze, according to Levinas, hinders the meeting with the Other's transcendence because it opens up to meaning only on the basis of the structure and features of objects (the green eyes, the pointed chin, the pursed lips). 'The look is knowledge, perception' and, in this sense, it is first of all, an act of grasping. 'Vision moves into grasp,' and it is thus not by chance that the gaze 'invites the hand to movement and to contact, and ensures them.' 'The forms of objects calls for the hand and the grasp,'[4] and the hand reaches out to the object and proceeds along the course that the gaze has already cleared for it and that, from the start, defines the return to the familiar borders of the self. The gaze is a forward surge whose aim is a return. The gaze grasps parts of the world and brings them back home, adapted to the basic structures and needs of consciousness. The gaze, then, remains subservient to the regime of the same, subject to a consciousness that remains within itself, within its own contents, a consciousness that zealously preserves closure as a condition of self-identity, without any possibility of opening up to a radical outside.

But what exactly is implied by this? Are the visual and the ethical sides of the face mutually exclusive? Is the face that concerns Levinas not the visible face? Levinas' own formulations do not always help: 'Not to notice the color of his eyes!' Is Levinas suggesting that we turn our back on the visual? Is it necessary, or indeed at all possible, to suspend seeing in order to turn to the face? This is not Levinas' point here, as his next sentence makes clear: 'The relation with the face can surely be dominated by perception, but what is specifically the face is what cannot be reduced to that.' What matters here then, is not so much the actual need to shut ourselves off to the input of vision, but rather how can we, in our visual life, resist the gaze's tendency to objectify the Other? How, within the realm of the gaze, can we evade the regime of the same?

Levinas' attitude to the visual remains ambivalent, not to say slightly hostile. As in the Old Testament and in rabbinic literature, a strong and insoluble tension prevails in Levinas' writing between the infinite (the divine) and what human eyes are capable of secing, what they are allowed to see. And yet, it merits attention that the ethical and the visual are not only not opposites, but that they are necessarily entwined. Indeed, for Levinas, 'ethics is an optics.' The visual dimension of the world is not merely an outer layer to be discarded but a fundamental aspect of human existence. To be in the world means to live at the intersection of seeing and been seen, to be part of a visual space whose characteristics are intimately connected to who we are (our identity, corporeality, sexuality at the personal, social, political, cultural levels). In this sense, the face too is always part of the visual space: there it breathes and, ultimately, only there can it be revealed.

And yet, the face of the Other is not part of the visual field simply as a given. The visual field is not only what allows the face to appear, but is also a realm of concealment. Surprisingly, the visible conceals. Yet, the issue here is not the concealment of something that could have shown itself to the eye. What is hidden in the visual space is a different type of fact: the very existence of what, in principle, cannot be made visible. The face is never in front of us, like a fruit bowl on the table or a sign on top of the building. But neither is it hidden, as a letter in a shoebox, nor is there something specific that conceals it, like a hand blocking a camera lens. So how *does* the face appear?

The entry of the face into the Levinasian philosophical picture is, as noted, methodologically significant. Beyond this, however, the modality of 'entering a picture' is essential to the face, and we may even say that the face is itself a kind of entry into a picture. The face, then, is not something that is simply there, positioned, placed, or given as such, but is always part of a becoming, involved in its own revelation. The face is part of a movement that unravels the mesh of the visual, but is not itself entwined in the visual web. The face erupts into the visible and leaves clear traces, but is never found in the visual field as the object of vision. The face comes to the visual from a beyond. While showing itself, breaking into the frame of the visual, the face never coalesces into a visual object. The face's form of appearance is not the form of a 'something' and, as such, it also eludes the network of visual concepts. In *Meaning and Sense*, Levinas writes:

> The manifestation of the other is, to be sure, produced from the first conformably with the way every meaning is produced. Another is present in a cultural whole and is illuminated by this whole, as a text by its context. The manifestation of the whole ensures his presence; it is illuminated by the light of the world. The understanding of the other is thus a hermeneutics and an exegesis. The other is given in the concreteness of the totality in which he is immanent ... But the epiphany of the other involves a signifyingness of its own independent of this meaning received from the world. The other comes to us not only out of the context, but also without mediation; he signifies by himself ... This presence consists in coming toward us, in *making an entry*. This can be put in this way: the *phenomenon* which the apparition of the other is also a *face* ... the epiphany of a face is a *visitation*.[5]

The face of the Other appears in the here and now. It has no other time or place. The Other, then, appears 'from the first' as 'every meaning.' 'The other is given in the concreteness of the totality in which he is immanent,' that is, he appears as someone specific, always within a social-cultural-political context, located in a network of given meanings, in an already present matrix of differences. 'The manifestation of the whole ensures his presence': what enables the Other to appear as possessing a particular and separate meaning is his specific location in the whole, the similarity to x and the difference from y. Yes, he was born here, but he has lived abroad since he started university. Yes, he comes every summer to visit, but he actually stopped coming when his parents died. Now he visits for other reasons. No, he's not married, but he was; he has a relationship, but the word ('relationship') is not something he would use and so forth.

To put it differently, when we meet another person, we tend to allow her – her actions, words, face, body, clothing – to be intelligible only as part of a given 'cultural context.' Levinas writes:

> Ordinarily … one is a 'character': a professor at the Sorbonne, a Supreme Court justice, son of so-and-so, everything that is in one's passport, the manner of dressing, of presenting oneself. And all signification in the usual sense of the term is relative to such a context.[6]

The usual meanings we ascribe to the Other's face are also created in this fashion: 'Why are you sad today?' 'I can see you're tired.' 'What is that smile?' Or, these are exactly Sophia Loren's eyes, or, what is that beard you've grown, what have you got to hide?

In the context of such horizons of meaning, our attitude to the other person is, as Levinas points out, fundamentally cognitive: 'The understanding of the other is thus a hermeneutics and an exegesis.' At the basis of the interaction with the other person, then, is our dynamic ability to interpret her, to locate her every time anew within a given matrix of differences, a context, a whole.

All this is precisely what does not take place in the ethical encounter with the Other, the encounter with her face: 'Here, to the contrary, the face is meaning all by itself.'[7] Or, to return to the passage cited above: 'But the epiphany of the other involves a signifyingness of its own independent of this meaning received from the world. The other comes to us not only out of the context, but also without mediation; he signifies by himself.' The meaning that opens up the alterity of the Other is of a unique order. Although the whole, or the totality, serves as its background and context, this meaning emerges, as if grounding itself, liberated from their authority.

But how is this possible? One clue to an answer may be Levinas' saying that the Other's 'presence consists in coming toward us, in *making an entry*.' Whereas usually and most of the time the Other's identity appears in the context of a world of sense that unfolds *in front of us*, the unique presence of the other is revealed precisely in its 'making an entry' into this world. The face of the Other is not an object. It is never found *there*, but is present in another way: it comes toward us. 'The epiphany of a face is a *visitation*.' Thus, although we are now sitting across each other at the table I cannot, according to Levinas, say where your face is located. The face is not something that I can frame with my camera or whose location I can point to because it is not located in any kind of 'there,' say, around the nose or in the front of the head that is leaning against the wall. Indeed, the very expression 'the face's location' or 'is located' is, in a deep sense, inappropriate here. The face is not located anywhere, at least not in the ordinary sense of things filling up a given space with their mass. Rather, the face is present as a kind of movement, the crossing of a border.

In Hebrew, as Levinas well knew, the root of the ancient biblical word *panim* (face) is a verb (*panah*) indicating, as I explain below, the movement – sometimes the action – of facing something, of addressing, of turning toward (*peniyya*). The unique presence of the face consists in such a turning. The face for Levinas is a one-directional vector traversing the space between you and I, the concretization of an original event that precedes any specific meaning that may appear and take form in the domain of sense.

The face is the original presence of the other person whose being is a turning to the I, a *facing* that is (ontologically) prior to any particular content of the speech or action of that person. The face of the Other attests to the existence of such a turning toward me, commanding me, calling upon me for a response and thus making me responsible, regardless of what has been said or of what I understand from what has transpired between us.

Let us now return to the question already posed. The face: are we speaking of a visual phenomenon? Is the face, as Levinas himself asks, 'given to vision?'[8] Levinas, as noted, has reservations about the very use of visual language to describe what concerns him in the human face. But given these reservations, his choice of a metaphor with such strong visual connotations could become problematic. In the less charitable interpretations of Levinas, this tension is indeed often a source of unease: is the use of the term 'face' concrete or metaphorical? And even if it is metaphorical, can it serve Levinas' aim at all? Is not the face, with all its warranted visuality, ultimately – as Derrida suggests – disruptive of Levinas' project?

The critique implied by this question is to a large extent internalized by Levinas in his later writings, where the image of the face loses prominence. Thus, whereas the face is at the core of *Totality and Infinity* (1961), it is entirely marginalized in his important work *Otherwise than Being* (1974). Levinas' renunciation of the face as 'a place' or 'an event' fundamental to his thought is related, inter alia, to his search for a new and more radical language that will release him from the fetters binding him to the phenomenological tradition. Despite his debt to it, phenomenology remains for Levinas a reflective framework that shuts itself off to the transcendent largely because it internalizes a concept of 'presence' rooted in visual perception. For various reasons, I take Levinas' understanding of the concept of phenomenological presence to be too narrow, but this is a subject that requires separate discussion. For my purposes here, what is important is to note that Levinas ultimately chooses to free his writing from the pervasive tension between visibility and invisibility that had initially shaped his thinking.

It should already be clear at this point that I do not think of the conceptual tension resonating in Levinas' use of the face as a problem to be solved or dissolved. Rather, I believe that it is important for our thinking to learn to live with this kind of tension, one that is not brought about by Levinas' concept of the face but is revealed and acquires resonance through this concept. Again, is the face that concerns Levinas the visible face? Answering this question in the affirmative would probably be incorrect, but a simple negative answer would not be right either. Searching for additional options, we may say, for example, that in being visible, the face is what cannot be seen. We could also capture the point by turning this sentence around: the face is seen in being invisible. It is seen as the invisible (but Levinas would probably not accept this formulation, which sounds too similar to the language of Merleau-Ponty).

Even if what is central in the face is not visual (as Levinas argues), this non-visuality is located at the very core of the visible. The ethical dimension has no other place to reveal itself and, in this sense, Levinas' use of the face cannot be understood without addressing the unique form of its visual presence. Even if the visuality of the face is not an end in itself for Levinas, it nevertheless provides the necessary access to what is ultimately sought after (the ethical). Your eyes, the wrinkle in your forehead, the hidden pinching of the lips: even if we wish to argue that one should not stop at them, they cannot be ignored either. They are a necessary stage, a window that must be there in order to be opened, in order for us to see through and recognize the abysmal and unbridgeable distance that hides in the few feet that separate us from one another. The image of the window does indeed recur in Levinas' works, such as when he writes:

> The other who manifests himself in a face as it were breaks through his own plastic essence, like a being who opens the window on which its own visage was already taking form. His presence consists in *divesting* himself of the form which does already manifest him.[9]

The face is the site of the Other's epiphany. Not only does the face break into my space as an observer, not only does it undermine the structure of the subject to which it turns (as will be explained), but its epiphany takes place through the unravelling of the visual fabric from which it emerges. What we have here is a breaking of the 'plastic essence,' a 'divesting of the form,' the opening of a window that has thus far allowed us, in being shut, to think of it mistakenly as the actual frame for the appearance of things. I look out the window. The window frame frames my field of vision and the windowpane functions as that field of appearance through which the outside manifests itself. Every point in my field of vision can be represented on the glass-pane, so that we could have actually argued that what is present now before me is not the outside itself but only a representation appearing on the window surface. Similarly, one could argue, as has indeed recurrently been done in the history of philosophy, that representation is the fundamental structure of our vision, that seeing is an internal, mental, framing of a picture. Thus, seeing a man, for example – let us say, seeing the man who is now getting out of the double-parked car across the street – amounts to holding a mental representation of that man.

Similar assumptions were also the basis of predominant conceptions of visual representation typical of the science of perspective in Renaissance painting. Thus, for example, when the Renaissance humanist Leon Battista Alberti develops in his book *On Painting* (1435) the principles of perspective that would allow painters to represent things 'as they appear,' he posits the transparent surface of a windowpane as a regulating model for understanding the picture surface. The windowpane is not only a framed transparency that allows the rays reflected from objects to reach our eye, but it is also in itself a medium of representation. Intersecting with the visual pyramid, it presents a full mapping of the visual field, creating a screen of appearances whose virtual double is the picture surface. Lacking any real depth, the picture surface – just like the window – opens up as if it were an actual visual field.[10]

The act of painting, according to Alberti, is thus a reconstruction of the visual givenness of things as they would appear were the painter to look at them through a window. And the window, like the painting, has a structure absolutely analogous to that of the realm of the visible, since it is, itself, a cross-section of the pyramid whose basis is the visual field. In this sense, the window is a surface that gives full perspectival expression to the field of vision and, as such, is the ground for virtual vision. The windowpane is the virtual duplicate of the visual space seen through it. But as such, it is also a sign of a danger constantly lurking in our encounter with the outside. Will we know how to differentiate the virtual from the real? How will we know, and will there still be a reason for preserving the difference between them? Can we possibly release ourselves from the hold of the virtual on our lives? Will we let our lives pass only on this, the inner side of the window, or will we find paths leading to real encounters with what is outside it?

I suggest that we understand Levinas' metaphor of the window in similar terms. According to him, others usually appears before us as if they were a two-dimensional image on a window pane. We meet the Other through a transparent partition that, because of its transparency, conceals the fact that this encounter is lacking a fundamental dimension. Ostensibly, the other person is right in front of us, fully there. And indeed, looking at him or listening to her through the window can teach us a great deal about the other person, perhaps even all there is to know. As spectators, nothing is allegedly hidden from us. We can, in principle, see, understand and explain just about everything, but what easily remains hidden in such a situation, when facing the window, is the fact that our encounter with the Other is actually 'encounterless.' For Levinas, the (closed) window functions as an image for an encounter with the Other that is confined to the reception of visual data or, more generally, of information that can only show itself to us, however precise and correct, in a depthless objectified form.

The substitution of the unique Other who turns to us in its two-dimensional representation, an object answering to the same description, is familiar to us from instances wherein we recognize how a person's objectification fails to respect his or her humanity, just as it also injures our humanity as observers: the Other as seen by the soldier at the roadblock; the gaze of the bureaucrat who sees the person facing them solely through the prism of their conformity to the criteria on the form, and the unbearable ease with which the doctor turns the patient into an anonymous bundle of symptoms. Our day-to-day life contains many examples of power-driven, objectifying, subjugating, erasing gazes. But such concrete cases seem to be of less concern to Levinas, perhaps because he thinks that ignorance of the Other is all too clear and obvious in them, and perhaps because he is primarily interested in the very structure of effacement that, for him, is found at every level of our interaction with others.

When Levinas deals with the violent indifference of the gaze or with its inherent closure to the Other, he speaks about the very structure of human communality, about fundamental patterns of our routine interaction with others that also – and perhaps first of all – includes friends, children, parents, siblings and neighbours. But can Levinas' claim remain so generalized, without committing itself to the specificity of particular cases? Is erasing the humanity of a foreign worker who is pushed into a prisoners' van equivalent to the flattening of the Other's otherness in the context of a conversation, even a fight, between friends? Can we begin to approach the question of alterity without taking account of the very specific social-political contexts in which the Other's alterity appears?

Returning to the window metaphor: to look at the Other's figure encoded on the surface of the window means, according to Levinas, to remain on one side of the glass, at home, within ourselves. Instead of responding to the Other, we open up (regardless of our intention or our knowledge) to the forms of representation through which we look at others. In contrast, as the face appears, a window opens up. The face is the opening of a window. But what appears through the window is not only another dimension of the same figure that had already shown itself on the windowpane. This is not only a 'thickening' of the visual image. Rather, the opening of the window involves, above all, a structural transformation: a change in the structure of our 'home' and, analogically, in the structure of the self. To live with an open window means to renounce the clear separation, the rigid distance between outside and inside. It means that the outside can call upon and visit the domestic space in rhythms of its own, like the rain, or like a butterfly, or like a thief in the night.

This transformation occurs together with the undermining of the familiar order of the visual. This is what Levinas calls the 'breaking of the plastic essence,' 'the divestment of form.' The Other's face attests to a dimension of the visual that cannot be gathered into the gaze and, as such, has no shape, lacks a plastic essence. The Other's face breaks the frontal structure of the visual field and, specifically, reveals to us the non-frontal presence of the Other.

To say that the relationships between self and Other are not frontal means that they are not mirror relations. Your face, as a turning toward me, is not a reflection of my gaze or my face turning to you. The ethical relationship that Levinas calls 'face to face' is not a symmetrical relationship (despite the implication apparent in the expression). Your face looks at me, turns to me now, but the essence of this turning dos not grow within the horizons of the I–You relationship.

This is a crucial point in Levinas' critique of the philosophy of Martin Buber, whose book *I and Thou* (1922) is an important influence on Levinas. Like Buber, Levinas ascribes crucial importance to the question of the possibility of a true encounter with the Other. The background for raising this question is a shared understanding of a fundamental problem implied by the structure of our openness to the world. And yet, Levinas opposes the kind of 'solution' suggested by Buber. In particular, he is opposed to Buber's articulation of the essence of our genuine openness to the Other in terms of a dialogical encounter, one resting on a primary relationship, a singular pre-cognitive proximity that enables the I to see through the objective characteristics of the other person and experience him or her directly as a 'Thou.'

The possibility of such an intimate closeness can be extremely comforting but should not be confused, according to Levinas, with openness to the Other's radical alterity. Buber's attempt to release the Other from the patterns of general, objective thought is, according to Levinas, worthy and important, but because it rests on a symmetrical articulation of interpersonal relationships, it inevitably falls into the frame of totality.[11] Buber's 'Thou' does escape the self's conceptual horizons, but its (non-conceptual) presence is nevertheless positioned as if it were embraceable by – sharing the same grounds as – the I. Contrary to Buber, Levinas searches for a way of formulating the Other's presence without presenting it as part of that shared space, that is, by preserving its strong transcendence. In this sense, the revelation of the face should not, according to Levinas, be seen as evidence of intimacy with the Other but rather as a trace of the infinite distance between us. The Other's face is not the close and frontal face of the Thou. Rather, it is, described by Levinas, in terms analogous to a grammatical third person: not Thou but the 'he,' always further away:

> The *beyond* from which a face comes is in the third person. The pronoun 'He' expresses its unexpressible irreversibility, already escaping every relation as well as every dissimulation, and in this sense absolutely unencompassable … The *illeity* of the third person is the condition for the irreversibility.[12]

Grammatically, the distinction between second and third person correlates with an understanding of two modalities of being in the space of linguistic interaction: while the second person is an active part of the self's space of language – frontally situated vis-à-vis the first person speaker – a third person is, in principle, an outsider to that space and, as such, cannot be addressed directly. Consequently, the face, while turning toward me, always remains outside the egological sphere. Levinas argues that the 'third person' analogy should be understood literally and unequivocally. The Other's presence is not of the kind that allows for a glimpse of the hidden to be revealed, but shows itself as what will never open up to us and will never be a home to us. Levinas explains that 'the illeity of the third person' is for him 'the condition for the irreversibility.' Thus, whereas the space of the I-Thou relationship allows us to put ourselves in one another's place, the 'he' points to a dimension that does not belong to the space of reciprocity. The 'he' is one to whom the laws of perspective do not apply as he is not at all part of the dynamic field of viewpoints wherein the self is anchored.

And thus, there is no way for the I to frame the presence of the Other, to review the 'he' from all directions, as we are so used to doing when we say, when a camera is at hand, 'Stand here. I want to look at you from there.' The 'he' can neither be brought closer to sight, nor can I ever see him fully from the side, from above or from below; he is 'absolutely unencompassable.'

Face 3
Face and Object

— It's right there, look!
— I can't see anything

The face of the Other tears the egoism of consciousness and exposes the ethical structure of the self. So Levinas tells us. But even if we recognize in the Levinasian suggestion an ethical possibility that we would wish to affirm, the option of making it part of our day-to-day life is not easy to envisage. What are the grounds for Levinas' claim? Is his claim anything more than wishful thinking? Perhaps a utopia? What is – or could be – the validity of the Levinasian idea? Is there any way of proving the validity of his claims? At the beginning of the third millennium, when force is everywhere and violence is both nearby and distant, when everything, micro and macro, is negotiable, commodified, instantly tailored and quickly disposed of: what should we look at, what can we look at in order to see for ourselves?

A beginning of an answer could still be found in our everyday experience. Although, at first glance, our usual encounters with the Other bear no trace of the unsettling transcendence that Levinas ascribes to the face, immediate experience is what provides, according to him, the setting for the face's epiphany. In this sense, Levinas should be understood as a phenomenologist whose strength is not so much a high capacity for abstraction but rather an ability to help us see what lies hidden in front of our eyes. Levinas offers nothing resembling a systematic argument, a proof, or an inference that could validate his claim about the infinity of the face or its power to resist the mechanisms of totality. What

43

he does do is point at aspects of the face's appearance that despite (and perhaps because) of their being part of what is always in front of us, remain concealed.

Wittgenstein writes that 'the aspects of things that are most important for us are hidden because of their simplicity and familiarity. One is unable to notice something – because it is always before one's eyes.'[1] Levinas' starting point, like Wittgenstein's, is the understanding that the structure of our everydayness is not simple; surprisingly, what is manifest and open may also conceal, and what shows itself to the eye may simultaneously remain hidden from it. Thus, the face can remain hidden from us precisely because it is in front of us, because the eye has become fixated on its relationship with it, and particularly because the gaze is locked in a frontal relationship with the face, a relationship that only allows it to see the face as a kind of object. This, as suggested, is one of Levinas' starting points: the face is not an object. Its appearance does not have the form of a specific 'something' bearing objective features and located there, in front of us, identical to itself. Like Merleau-Ponty, who writes that true philosophy consists in 'relearning to look at the world,'[2] Levinas also attempts to teach a new vision. Levinas neither wishes to nor can prove the claim that the face is not an object; in obvious ways, it is certainly an object. His intent, rather, is to enable us to recognize the sense in which the face transcends its objective structures, the senses in which the face does not belong to the general order of the meaning of things (or, in a formulation that belongs to another tradition, the senses in which God may be said to be present in the face).

In order to understand what distinguishes the face from the object, we may begin by framing the object as a 'some-thing': it is not only 'this and that' but also 'this and no other.' To appear as something specific is to be intelligible. The object has, or possesses, meaning and, furthermore, it becomes meaningful through the display of this possessive structure. The object is intelligible in that it is the organizing form of given possibilities of sense. The car is fast; the building is tall; the sweet is tasty. The object is not, in itself, an origin or an event of meaning, but a structure that delimits and determines meaning and thus enables it to appear – it is a kind of frame through which different units of meaning, whose point of intersection is the particular 'something,' can become manifest: this object is metallic, it is dark, it is on the table.

The meaning of the object emerges when the object presents to the eye a set of inner links that it upholds and displays there, in front of us. The object is what it is and, at the same time, the fact of its appearance as such does not depend only on the inner relationships revealed within it. What allows the object to appear as itself is its belongingness to a broader matrix of relationships within which the particularity of the meaning-frame that it presents acquires clear contours. Thus, the object invariably appears against some background: it needs a background in order to be an object and, moreover, it invariably appears 'among' and 'in between,' always at the heart of a multiplicity of objects and as part of more inclusive networks of meaning, whose place in them determines its significance.

According to Levinas, the appearance-structure of the object is essential to the visual field which unfolds by lending itself to a human gaze that frames what it sees. The object is vision's basic unit of content. And, vision, for Levinas, is thus a modality of engaging with the appearance of sense that is regulated by one predominant form of meaning which is always already framed, sealed, 'packaged' – that is, basically fitting the spectator's capacity for containment. To see means to be directed to what is already located in a differential matrix of possibilities that, from the spectator's perspective, share the same basic structure. The gaze turns, for instance, to the house across the street: is it one or two stories high? Three or four? Tall windows or narrow openings? New, old, well looked after, neglected, sun-filled, dark? The case is always such and such.

Levinas' conceptualization of vision and the visual is, in itself, quite narrow and limited. And of particular interest in this context is the extent of his indifference to contemporary philosophical moves (such as Merleau-Ponty's) which he knew well and which explicitly concern the inexhaustible depths of the visual. Contrary to the way Merleau-Ponty's phenomenology teaches us to recognize the 'invisible' as an essential dimension of the visual itself, for Levinas the visual seems to remain entirely frontal and positivistically flat. The one exception admitted by Levinas is, as suggested, the face to which he ascribes the unsealing and rupturing of the visual.

Whereas Merleau-Ponty seeks to uncover a layer of vision that is more primary than the representation of objects – and, in fact, one that releases the entire realm of the visible from the rule of the object – Levinas seemingly accepts the working assumption that vision is equivalent to the representation of objects. It is against the background of this understanding that he also argues for the need to recognize an exceptional or extraordinary 'place' within the visual: the face is indeed that unique place that opens up to the gaze in a way incompatible with the rule of the object. 'The appearance in being of these "ethical peculiarities" – the humanity of man – is a rupture of being.'[3] But can this visual 'exception' ultimately create a change in our understanding of the entire visual realm?

A central theme in Levinas' attempt to differentiate the appearance of the face from the appearance of the object touches on the singularity he ascribes to the face. Unlike the object, the face is, before anything else, singular; it is *the* singular. Being singular, in the full sense of the term, means to be single, ostensibly one of a kind. But the expression 'one of a kind' is not really pertinent here because it involves an inner tension: by the very fact of being one of a kind, any kind, the singularity of the one cannot be absolute because, by definition, it already assumes a shared unity in the multiplicity. The strong singularity of the face (yours, for instance) means, for Levinas, that it does not belong to a *genus*, not even to the general kind 'face.' The face is the manifestation of what appears as itself only from within itself.

Whereas 'the meaning of something is in its relation to another thing,'[4] the face lacks a context: it is not similar, not different and not dependent on the general order of sense. As such, one could indeed say that the face embodies a utopia, not because it is in some way ideal but because the literal sense of the term resonates within it. That is, although the face is entirely concrete, showing itself between us, here and now, it has no place in what appears in front of us: the space of the frontal. The face is not to be found on the map of the visual. It is a no-place. Driving a car, a man absorbed in a map or a GPS may unexpectedly raise his gaze only to see a bird or a treetop in the wind; the face thus suspends the general order within which the gaze operates. It opens up to us without allowing our gaze to return to itself, to locate itself as it is used to and knows how to do.

We could also say that what breaks through in the face is what cannot be replaced, what neither has nor could have a substitute. Confronted with your face, for example, I become a witness to the existence of an abysmal singularity that has no measure and that cannot be compared to anything, even though it is located at the very heart of a realm of comparisons and alternatives. 'Shall I compare thee to a summer's day?' Often, when in love or when losing a beloved face, this type of vision becomes sharper. Is the uniqueness of a thing, its singularity, fundamentally connected to its being transient? To the fact that loss is inseparable from the horizon of experiencing it?

For Levinas, the singularity of the face is a dimension that lends itself to our seeing, insofar as the word 'seeing' or 'vision' is appropriate (or better, inappropriate) here. The singularity of the face is constantly present in front of us. And thus, even if we are generally indifferent to the singular, Levinas' starting point is that we can, in principle, learn to recognize and open up to its presence. Without a sensitivity and, perhaps, a new sensibility regarding the singular, there is hardly room to go any further with Levinas. And yet, we neither do nor ever could have a recipe for developing such sensitivity. The singular has no measure and, therefore, it always concedes to schematic thought, losing itself when attempts are made to locate it within a frame of reference.

The singular can show itself only when it is free from the burden of the frame. Allowing the singular to appear would thus require that we learn how to suspend the world, push out the horizon, learn how to meet it on its own.

Face 4
Why a Face, All of a Sudden?

Conceptually, the face is a crossroads, a seam line, an open meaning that cannot be bound, an unsolved question. Phenomenologically, the face is, first of all, a call of sorts, one arriving from the outside, preceding any particular content, image, or spectacle, any specific visual configuration. The face calls me – it addresses the I; it comes to me, confronts me before I have even taken a first step, before I have begun making preparations for a meeting. The face is one step ahead. It is an unexpected guest, a doorbell ringing all of a sudden. The face is the unexpected. Preceding form, it is *all* of a sudden.

Face, Unfinished List

Tony Soprano, Yonit from Channel 2, Nasarallah, Ehud Olmert, Morris the grocer, Jonathan, Dürer – self-portrait 1500, drawing from 1492, a mirror in the passage (I), Mom, Dad 1961 (the Alps), 1966 (on the city's wall in Acre), 72' (Los Angeles), then 1997 (in the garden with I–L.), 2006 Mom (by the table with friends, I try to do something with it using Photoshop), Holbein's Ambassadors, the Darmstadt Madonna, Mao Tse Tung, Marilyn Monroe, Marlon Brando, Che Guevara, Lenin, Yossi, Carmel (from Café George), Vered (now, music in the background), Emil (feeding a cat), Grandma, Illu, Noa, Renush, Neta, Avi, Liora, Tutti, Sarah P., Wittgenstein (on a cover), Heidegger, Schopenhauer (cover, cover),

49

David Hockney, Dichter, Chico Menashe, an eyewitness, a judge, Dana, Eilam, Eli, Inbar (lower), Van Gogh (bandage), Van Gogh (light blue background), Francis Bacon, Parmigianino (in a convex mirror), Mor, Moran, Maurice Natanson, Lois (his wife), Lewis G., Ezra Pound (website), Richard Gere, M. Begin, Ben-Gurion, Bush, Putin, Merkel, Zidane, Ronaldo, Ronaldinho, Ribéry, Franz Beckenbauer, Johan Cruyff, Nadine, Shlomo, Shlomo Artzi, Nissim, Zehavah, Daliah, Emily, Vinnie, Efrat, Dov, Mickey Berkowitz, Tal Brody, Yeruham Meshel, Peretz, Peres, Shoshi, Sarah, Nitzah, Gabi, Dad, Freud, Lucian Freud, Karsten, Nicholas, Nicolas Cage, Janis Joplin, Bob Dylan (Freewheeling), then Desire (and then the opening interview in Scorsese's movie), Scorsese himself, Harvey Keitel, Robert De Niro, Al Pacino (young, the Godfather, old?), Orson Welles, Roland Barthes, Nastassja Kinski, Orit (Illu's teacher), Oren, Zohar, Meret Oppenheim, Giacometti, Erez Elul, Michael L., Michael S. C., Assi, Woody Allen, Juliette Lewis, Juliette Greco, Johnny Depp, Brad Pitt, Charlie Chaplin, Steven Spielberg, Bill Gates, Ninette, Assi Dayan, Assi Dayan's son, Assi Dayan's father Moshe Dayan, Dov, Liat, Nir, Tsahi Hanegbi, Geula Cohen, Shulamit Aloni, Aryeh Meliniak, Avot Yeshurun, Max Ernst, Subidah, John Goodman, Derrida, Dean Martin, Steve Martin, Napoleon, Borges, Jesus (Bellini), the cook at Ginsburg, Seinfeld, Kramer, Gabriel Preil, Lior Carmi (child and adult), Vivien Leigh, Rhett Butler, John Ford, John Huston, Anjelica Huston, Larry Bird, Karim Abdul Jabbar, Eli Stern, Eli's mother, Michael Jordan, Michael Jackson, Michael Halberstam, Kate, Max, Anna, Mimi, Leon Blum, Ron, Joanna, Adam, Keanu Reeves, Meirav, Andrea, Mr Spock (intergalactic voyage), Yitzhak Rabin, Mota Gur (Azit the paratrooper dog?), Julius Caesar (at the national museum), Fayoum woman with a hint of a smile, James Bond – Sean Connery, James Bond – Roger Moore, James Bond – a…, Dr No, Batman, Superman, Jack Nicholson, Charlie Brown, Brigitte Bardot, Liza Minnelli, Sophia Loren, Hitchcock, Bertrand Russell, Sartre, Edith Piaf, Hava Alberstein, Arik Einstein, Albert Einstein, Picasso, Paloma, Dora Maar, Casals (programmes in educational television), Andy Warhol, Grace Jones, Howard Stern, Jean Gabin, Jean Moreau, Anna Magnani, Fellini, Giulietta Masina, Truffaut, Depardieu, a taxi driver with vitiligo (today), Taxi Driver De Niro, an employee at Galassi, Giddy, Joel, Leonard, Leonardo (Da Vinci?), Leonardo DiCaprio, Jimmy Stewart, Edna, Kate Bush, Joni Mitchell, Roosevelt, Russell, Virginia Woolf, Sarah Brodie, Thierry (an unexpected mail).

Face 5
Vision, Gaze, Other

Two different questions intersect in Levinas' concept of the face, both fundamental to the phenomenological tradition that is its cradle. The one is the question of vision: what is seeing? What is the essence of vision and of visuality? What is a visual phenomenon? What is the character of visual experience? In the present context, this could be called the 'question of optics.' The second question has an ethical resonance: it concerns the appearance or the phenomenal presence of the human Other: does the Other appear to consciousness in any unique way? How does the Other's subjectivity show itself? Can consciousness access the Other's subjectivity? What kind of presence is distinctive of the human? Does the appearance of the Other differ – and if so, in what way – from that of an object? In the merging of these two questions, a third one opens up: what kind of visual experience is implied in the encounter with the other person? Can the otherness of the other person take on any visual form? What kind of visual presence does it have? What does it mean to see a person as a person (as opposed to seeing a tree or a machine)? What does it mean to see the other person as an Other? What do I see when I see you?

Unlike the consistent preoccupation of the history painting, and portraiture in particular, with the phenomenality of the human figure, philosophy has been generally uninterested in exploring the visual dimension of the human as a theme in and of itself. For philosophy, the question of the visibility of the individual never appears on its own and emerges only in the context of broader questions. This is also the case in the works of Husserl and Sartre, who provide the immediate philosophical background for Levinas' move.

Levinas and Husserl

In *Cartesian Meditations*, a text that influenced the young Levinas, who was also one of its French translators, Husserl poses the question of the Other's phenomenality in new, unprecedented terms. The framework of the discussion indeed remains bound by the epistemological question about the existence of other minds, but this motivation leads Husserl to an analysis of the concrete modalities of the Other's givenness to consciousness that, in many ways, is more interesting than Husserl's conclusive demonstration. The need to deal with the question of Other's appearance emerges in the context of Husserl's attempt to answer 'what may seem to be a grave objection. The objection concerns nothing less than the claim of transcendental phenomenology to be itself transcendental *philosophy*';[1] that is, a philosophy that discloses the primary conditions that precede the actual structures of consciousness and make human experience possible.

Husserl understands his method as a new possibility of uncovering a transcendental layer in the ego's experience of the world, even while recognizing that his call for philosophy's immersion in the ego's field of experience gives rise to a problem of method:

> When I, the meditating I, reduce myself to my absolute transcendental ego by phenomenological epoché do I not become *solus ipse*; and do I not remain that, as long as I carry on a consistent self-explication under the name phenomenology?[2]

What troubles Husserl, then, is the validity of the intentional analysis that he himself had proposed. Could his phenomenology be trapped, despite its pretension of dealing with the 'things themselves,' within the limits of subjective consciousness? Husserl seeks to show why his phenomenology does not ultimately collapse into subjectivism or solipsism. And, in this respect, the idea of grounding the existence of what is in principle exterior to consciousness in the Other's form of givenness is critical for his entire phenomenological project.

Husserl attempts to dispel the threat of solipsism by showing that, even at 'zero level,' the ego's intentional experience never consists only of a substratum of private experiences but is always part of an intersubjective world. He wishes to show that the very core of consciousness, at the level of immanent contents, it already consists of what necessarily transcends it. For this purpose, he asks us to

> obtain for ourselves insight into the explicit and implicit intentionality wherein the alter ego becomes evinced and verified in the realm of our transcendental ego; we must discover in what intentionalities, syntheses, motivations, the sense 'other ego' becomes fashioned in me and, under the title, 'harmonious experience of someone else', becomes verified as existing and even as itself there in its own manner.[3]

Husserl demonstrates the evident uniqueness of the 'harmonious experience of someone else' by relying on an analysis of the thick intentional texture through which the Other appears. His analysis thus focuses on those dimensions of the alter ego's presence that cannot be understood in terms of a relationship with an object. He aims to show that, despite the apparent similarities between the appearance of the Other and that of the object in the field of consciousness, the presence of a human Other necessarily creates a gap, a distance that consciousness cannot bridge and, therefore, must learn to recognize and leave room for. The Other, as another subject, will always appear to consciousness through a dimension of absence. Husserl tries to teach his readers how 'to see' this absence, invariably present at the heart of the positive characteristics of the Other's appearance. This is a dimension lacking the form of a 'something' – it is a 'some-non-thing' – woven into the movements of the other person's body, gait, speech, acts, or face expressions. The Other, qua Other, is not positively present on the phenomenal surface that meets the eye but is experienced as the vanishing point of the visual field framed by the perceiving eye. Whoever does not understand this will never be able to discover the Other's presence in the visual field.

To see another person necessarily means seeing more than what you see. What concerns Husserl in the 'Fifth Meditation' is indeed the decoding of those mechanisms of 'actualization' and 'presentification' that enable consciousness to see more than it seemingly sees. Husserl focuses on specific structures of intentionality, on unique kinds of syntheses that open up the possibility of experiencing the Other's subjectivity for consciousness, even if this subjectivity will never fully become an object of consciousness. But what is ultimately important to Husserl is the justification, the evidence that he finds in the structure of the Other's absent presence for arguing that consciousness is essentially open beyond itself. For him, the Other is the bridge between the interiority and exteriority of consciousness: while appearing as the content of consciousness, the other ego concomitantly reveals itself as consciousness' – irreducible – exteriority. Hence, when summing up, Husserl regards himself as successful in finding 'within' consciousness itself the key that liberates it from solipsistic closure and can thus conclude with the understanding that his 'actual explications have dissipated the [solipsistic] objection as groundless.'[4] He writes:

> What I demonstrate to myself harmoniously as 'someone else'
> and therefore have given to me, by necessity and not by choice,
> as an actuality to be acknowledged, is *eo ipso* the existing

Other for me in the transcendental attitude: the alter ego demonstrated precisely within the experiencing intentionality of my ego. Within the bounds of positivity we say and find it obvious that, in my own experience, I experience not only myself but others – in the particular form: experiencing someone else … 'In' myself I experience and know the Other; in me he becomes constituted – appresentatively mirrored, not constituted as the original. Hence it can very well be said, in a broadened sense, that the ego acquits – that I, as the one who meditatingly explicates, acquire by 'self-explication' (explication of what I find in myself) every transcendency: as a transcendentally constituted transcendency and not as a transcendency accepted with naïve positivity. Thus the *illusion* vanishes: that everything *I*, qua transcendental ego, *know as existing in consequence of myself*, and explicate as *constituted in myself*, must *belong to me as part of my own essence.*[5]

What merits attention here is that Husserl offers the young Levinas a theoretical model for the understanding of the relationship with the Other and that this model prefigures, despite Levinas' ambivalence toward it, several of the elements that will eventually become central in his later works. As suggested, Levinas explicitly acknowledges Husserl's influence, but no less important for him is the need to detach himself from what he understands as the crucial limitations of the Husserlian system. Husserl, according to Levinas, clearly paves the way for a unique metaphysical understanding of the relationship with the Other. First, he succeeds in identifying and articulating what is so clear, but also so blurred and indeterminate in the encounter with the Other: the phenomenological presence of the human other is absolutely unique. Yet, while the presence of a person in my field of vision is essentially different and, therefore, irreducible to the object's frame of appearance, it cannot be understood only in contrast to the object. The Other has a singular kind of presence that, according to Husserl, requires not only special handling but also an alternative philosophical sensibility, expressed in the ability to accept the philosophical contact with what cannot be grasped, with what invariably escapes when we insist on holding on to it. Husserl, then, is the one who links the appearance of the Other to a dimension of transcendence that belongs to the very heart of consciousness.

Reflecting on the human face, Levinas clearly builds upon Husserlian insights, but as he develops as an independent philosopher, the 'dialogue' he conducts with his teacher becomes increasingly critical. For him, Husserl's analysis of the Other's mode of givenness is ultimately subservient to the totality of consciousness. Husserlian consciousness is thus defined by him as, in principle, self-sufficient, discovering within itself not only the whole wide world but also the transcendent. In this sense, even if the human Other is indeed granted special status among consciousness' contents, its very belongingness to consciousness allows the appearing Other to be only an internal indication, a mark of the possibility of transcendence, and never an actual revelation of the reality of an absolute outside. In Husserl, according to Levinas, the Other's transcendence loses its radical essence because it is mediated to begin with. Husserl, then, construes the transcendence of the Other in a manner that, in principle, invalidates its radicalism. Ultimately, the Other is not allowed to transcend the limits of consciousness' containability. The Other's presence thus remains grounded, despite its uniqueness, in consciousness' terms of perception.

Husserl could not offer a rejoinder on this point, and it remains open whether Levinas' interpretation of Husserl's understanding of the 'experience of the stranger' succeeds in doing justice to his position. Furthermore, Levinas also tends to disregard a question that Husserl would certainly pose to him, as Derrida later did, concerning the very possibility of making room, in philosophical terms, for radical transcendence. Is not the Levinasian manner of introducing radical transcendence into philosophical discourse a contradiction in terms? Is not the very attempt to conceptualize transcendence already a betrayal of the uncontainable essence of the transcendent? Is this any more than a fantasy that, philosophically, could never be realized?

The distance separating Levinas and Husserl finds distinct phenomenological expression in Levinas' response to two further aspects of Husserl's analysis of the Other's presence. For Husserl, as suggested, the question of the Other calls us to 'discover in what intentionalities, syntheses, motivations, the sense "other ego" becomes fashioned in me and, under the title, harmonious experience of someone else.' Even if we leave open the question of whether such a formulation can, in principle, make room for the Other's radical transcendence, note that Husserl understands the experience of the Other as essentially harmonious.

This is a dominant and recurrent theme in Husserl's conception of meaning. For him, the task of describing the processes of constitution and synthesis of meaning typically presupposes, as in the case of the appearance of the alter ego, that the genesis and formation of meaning in the field of experience is a harmonious process. Meanings emerge, appear, and establish themselves when the constant multiplicity and change that are part of the stream of consciousness gather and coalesce around more or less clear and stable structures. These noematic structures, always dynamic and open to change, are essentially structures of harmony, consistency, and compatibility, of successful melding and coherence.

At the street corner, for example, as the bus turns right revealing two girls on a pedestrian crossing, I identify him in the crowd: 'But what is he doing in the country? ... When did he grow hair like that? And what is that suit?' the sunlight is blinding, 'Is it really him?' Yes, that's my old friend. In the Husserlian world – the world of meaning or of consciousness – the appearance of things is described as a taking on of form, a perpetual movement of coalescence into conscious solidity.[6] The encounter with the other person is understood in these same terms – that is, 'under the title, harmonious experience of someone else.'

But this is precisely what is rejected by Levinas, who identifies in the encounter with the Other a movement in the opposite direction. To put this in Husserlian terms, what takes place in the encounter with the face of the Other is a strong unravelling, a fracturing of the noematic structure. Whereas Husserl goes on thinking of the Other in the general terms of constitution and synthesis, Levinas points to a dimension of uncontrolled, unorganized, non-synthetic upsurge, a wound. The encounter with the Other is essentially disharmonious; not an uncovering of what lies within the horizons of consciousness but a revelation of what forces itself upon consciousness, doing so without 'asking for permission,' without taking consciousness into consideration, that is, in a manner that resists any kind of conformity with given forms of thought.

Disharmony is a crucial dimension of our experience of the Other, a dimension that would nevertheless remain inconspicuous in an understanding of the stream of experience guided solely by an ideal of harmony. 'A face imposes itself upon me without my being able to be deaf to its call or to forget it.'[7] With Husserl, however, there is yet a further reason we cannot 'hear' the strangeness of this call and cannot recognize how it subverts any shared configuration of meaning: Husserl is impervious to the radical disharmonious alterity of the Other because his investigation presupposes, to begin with, the kind of structure that would count as the basis for the Other's appearance. The basic assumption of the Husserlian inquiry is that the form of the Other's appearance is that of an alter ego, another-I. The Other, in Husserl, is another ego, an I who is not I.

Hence, while making a point of the need to account for the ways exterior consciousnesses give themselves to the 'I,' Husserl takes for granted that the structure of these exterior consciousnesses must be symmetrical and analogous to the I's consciousness. His inquiry is entirely focused on the question of how a given consciousness could open itself up to the presence of an exterior consciousness. At the basis of this question, however, is not the alterity of the other consciousness but rather the external location – the exteriority – of one consciousness vis-à-vis the other. The problem that concerns Husserl, then, is one pertaining to the multiplicity of consciousnesses and the conditions enabling such multiplicity so that, from his perspective, these consciousnesses can in principle be identical while clearly differing in their location in space. In this sense, according to Levinas, even when explicitly dealing with transcendence Husserl cannot make actual room for the Other's *alterity* because the alter ego remains, for him, essentially analogical to the ego.

Hence, it is already at the phenomenological level that Husserl, according to Levinas, fails to offer an adequate description of the phenomenon of otherness. What a rigorous analysis would show, in Levinas' view, is that the appearance of the Other is, at heart, disharmonious, attesting to a total incompatibility between the ego's gaze and the Other captured by this gaze. The encounter with the Other is exposed as a mismatch and, as such always bears the resonance of an excess that refuses to surrender to the gaze, a transcendence that cannot be contained by the gaze because it disrupts the formal stability of the intentional object as well as the continuity of the ego. The encounter described by Levinas is thus not a meeting with an intimate or twin soul, not a mirroring of the self in another I, not mutual acceptance or recognition but vulnerability, an unclear mixture of strength and weakness; passivity, dissonance, event.

Levinas and Sartre

Levinas' starting point is the insistence for the need to detach the phenomenon of the Other from consciousness' processes of synthetic constitution, as well as for the need to acknowledge a fundamental difficulty inherent in the encounter with the Other's face. These aspects of his thought develop in direct relationship with Sartre's discussion of the gaze and the encounter with the Other. For Sartre, the traditional formulation of the question of the Other's existence is symptomatic of a problematic mode of thinking that, ultimately, refuses to accept intersubjectivity as fundamental to the human condition. For him, the existence of others is such a clear philosophical starting point that he views traditional attempts to prove this existence as evidence of a crucial misunderstanding regarding the fundamental rootedness of the Other's presence in our lives. Consequently, like Levinas, Sartre's response to Husserl is also, at the very least, ambivalent.

> When Husserl in his *Cartesian Meditations* ... attempts to refute solipsism, he believes that he can succeed by showing that a referral to the Other is the indispensable condition for the constitution of a world ... For Husserl the world as it is revealed to consciousness is inter-monadic. The Other is present in it not only as a particular concrete and empirical appearance but as a permanent condition of its unity and of its richness ... these views show progress over the classical positions.[8]

While explicitly acknowledging the novelty of the Husserlian move, Sartre is also critical of Husserl who, in his view, remains bound by the epistemological tradition and by the barren expectation to turn the hypothetical status of the Other into a 'direct givenness,'[9] a certainty. Sartre regards the Husserlian intuition whereby absence is the very form of the Other's presence as a true achievement. Yet, he also holds that, since Husserl's intentional analysis does not allow the specificity of this absence to be made present in positive ways, it ultimately fails when confronting solipsism.

For Sartre, the unique Husserlian intentionality directed toward an absence is in fact an empty intentionality. 'The Other is the empty noema which corresponds to my directing toward the Other.'[10] That is, Husserl's phenomenological description is not an answer to the epistemological problem but only its recapitulation in other terms. The use of the term 'absence' does indeed disclose a dimension inherent in the Other's presence but, in itself, all that this term does is indicate that, beyond the objective givenness of the Other's corporality, the Other's subjectivity remains essentially inaccessible to the perceiving consciousness. For Sartre, the gap between the Other's subjectivity and the Other's givenness as an object of consciousness is, in principle, unbridgeable. We cannot derive from the contents (the objects) of consciousness the existence of something whose essential structure is not objective. And thus, framed as an object, the subjectivity of the Other – the existence of another consciousness beyond the mask of the face and the body – ineluctably betrays its essence and appears as a merely conjectural objectivity.

Nevertheless, the impossibility of extracting the certainty of the Other's existence from the object of consciousness and, specifically, from what appears to the eye, does not wholly negate the philosophical possibility of directly recognizing the Other's existence. All we can learn from this impossibility, according to Sartre, is that the tradition (of which Husserl is part) has failed to locate the relevant realm of experience wherein the Other's original presence shows itself unequivocally. Consequently, our task is to overcome this traditional misunderstanding of the way in which the Other, as Other, is revealed: a misunderstanding as to the kind of immediate experience wherein the Other is directly present.

Thus, while rejecting the possibility of meeting the Other's subjectivity through our visual perception, Sartre points to a unique form of daily experience wherein the immediate and unquestionable presence of other subjects is revealed: we are exposed to the presence of the Other when we ourselves are the object of their gaze, when we occupy a place in the Other's field of vision. In other words, we recognize the Other's subjectivity not by virtue of our vision, but by virtue of our visibility; not by seeing but by being seen.

The existence of the Other as a subject cannot assume its validity from the contents of our gaze but only through the experience of finding ourselves caught in the Other's gaze. That is, the Other's existence becomes self-evident to us as we are being looked at. To be an object of the Other' gaze is a primary and irreducible experience that Sartre understands as the phenomenological key to any further analysis of inter-subjective relations.

Hence, despite its importance, the philosophical focus on the intentional structure tends to conceal, according to Sartre, a dimension of passivity that is fundamental to the experiential field. The perceiving consciousness is also a perceived consciousness. Casting its net onto the world, consciousness frames a totality of objects that make up its world but, in so doing, consciousness is itself caught in the nets cast by other consciousnesses. It consequently experiences a traumatic fixation through the actual grip of the object-structure that the Other imposes upon it. In Sartre's view, the Other is revealed in the petrifying gaze of Medusa; the meaning of the Other's gaze is a concrete threat to my being a subject.

In presenting the gaze as an active vector in the public space, Sartre liberates vision from its traditional role as a receptive, containing medium, as a kind of mirror always placed outside the situation it represents. Vision, according to Sartre, is not an event unfolding behind the eyes and within the head. It is not an inner relationship between subject and image, between consciousness and its private contents, but a dimension of our existence in the actual, interpersonal world. Prior to framing any inner representation, vision already has an exterior effect. Before anything else, then, the visual field where the Other appears is a field of power, a living space of action and interaction, of clashing forces whose dynamism is grounded in struggle. 'Conflict is the original meaning of being-for-others,'[11] and the gaze is the initial experiential manifestation of this meaning, the paradigm epitomizing this conflict.

Others are present through the very power they exert over me, a power that disturbs the serenity, the indifference and, indeed, the self-sufficiency of my subjectivity. The gaze of the Other does not merely grasp the I – it always catches it 'red-handed,' necessarily reducing the existence of the self, the inner moments of the I, to a given pattern of facts. The gaze of the Other fixates the facticity of the self, the movements, the actions, the words, places them under an uncaring public light, indifferent to the flow of the self's inner life – like the flash in a photo booth or an identity parade, or like a *paparazzo* picture. Under the Other's gaze, the self finds itself 'in the street,' 'kicked out of its home,' forcibly thrown into a shallow public sphere of one-dimensional facts, of meanings and distinctions it does not control. Under the gaze, the self is no more than what is said of it: regardless of one's intentions, the significance of one's actions is determined by what is captured by the Other's gaze. You thought you were funny and special, but in her eyes you are just boring and vapid or petty and vulgar. You were convinced your feelings were sincere and unique, but the Other's gaze made it obvious that you are altogether a cliché. The rule of the gaze dismisses the privileged validity that the self ascribes to the nuances of its inwardness, to the invisible depths of the soul, to concealed intentions, to ambiguity or to its indeterminate grounds. The gaze of the Other

> holds ... the secret of what I am ... the Other's look fashions my body ... sculptures it, produces it as it is, *sees* it as I shall never see it ... He makes me be, and thereby he possesses me.[12]

Subjugating my subjectivity to the yoke of the object, the Other's gaze is an unbearable burden. 'Hell is other people,' and the only possible rescue from this binding condition is the counter enslavement of the Other. To be released from the gaze of the Other, I must 'turn back upon the Other so as to make an object out of him in turn since the Other's object-ness destroys my object-ness for him.'[13]

For Sartre, the gaze is a one-directional objectifying force that bifurcates the human involvement in the interpersonal encounter into two mutually exclusive possibilities: the Sartrean visual field determines an either-or situation in which gazes can neither meet nor reciprocate. Hence, when confronting the Other, the self is necessarily either subject or object. In this respect, the objectifying gaze that reveals the Other to me is precisely the one threatening my existence as subject. Since my relation with the Other is necessarily concretized in one of the two modes of visuality (either to see or to be seen), 'my reaction to my own alienation for the Other ...

[is] expressed in my grasping the Other as an object.'[14] For Sartre, then, the appearance of the Other is intrinsically connected to an analysis of the essence of the relationship between self and Other and, more specifically, to the insoluble struggle underlying every interpersonal dynamic:

> Everything which may be said of me in my relations with the Other applies to him as well. While I attempt to free myself from the hold of the Other, the Other is trying to free himself from mine; while I seek to enslave the Other, the Other seeks to enslave me.[15]

The Other is a constant and concrete threat to the ego's subjectivity. The Other divests the self of its subjective depth, of the latency of its inner life and, in that sense, the appearance of the Other is in no way part of the realm of representation but rather of the realm of power. The meeting of self and Other makes no room for a turning toward the Other nor does it open up any intermediate space between the Other and I. One could in fact say that, for Sartre, there really is no encounter with the Other but only the experience of being given over to the Other, of finding oneself under the steamrolling power of the Other's gaze. At the same time, and precisely because of the opposition between the order of power and the cognitive essence of consciousness, the other subject always remains – despite the contact with the self – entirely external to consciousness.

Levinas' explicit references to Sartre are usually critical. His critique targets the pugnacity that Sartre ascribes to the encounter between self and Other as well as the Sartrean dialectical structure, the dialectic of the gaze that, according to Levinas, cannot ultimately allow for any strong sense of transcendence. Unlike Sartre, Levinas argues that the face of the Other looks at me, turns toward me in a manner hiding an infinity that refuses to be contained in the gaze I return. No principle of mutuality or reciprocity is to be found here. Nor does this encounter involve any other dialectic (of containment and enslavement or of recognition and acceptance) that could bring our gazes together in becoming 'moments,' stages in a shared structure of higher unity.

Given Levinas' critique of Sartre, it merits note that, at least at a structural level, he is still strongly influenced by the Sartrean insight and, above all, by the inversion of the intentionality structure that enables Sartre to present the appearance of the Other in terms of the passivity of the self. For Levinas, Sartre models the possibility of thinking about the way consciousness opens up to the existence of the Other as a subject without subordinating this openness to the representational modality by which consciousness engages an entire world of contents. It is not through a domination of the visible that Sartrean consciousness encounters the other subject, but precisely because of its being vulnerable, a victim, thrown into a violent situation whose scope it cannot frame. The Other is made present to consciousness not because of what consciousness can represent to itself – contents – but because of the manner in which it is affected, that is, the situation into which it stumbles, its very transformation into an object. The Other's subjectivity is what consciousness can only be hurt by, but never contain. And, in this respect, when Levinas seeks ways of articulating the exteriority of the Other, the Sartrean model is unquestionably in his mind.

'The encounter with the Other in Sartre,' he writes, 'threatens my freedom, and is equivalent to the fall of my freedom under the gaze of another freedom.'[16] As suggested, Levinas' pacifist vision stands in direct opposition to such a confrontational understanding of the Other's gaze. And yet, and perhaps precisely because he too is preoccupied with the manner in which the Other's presence disrupts the solidity of the ego, Levinas must differentiate himself from Sartre by explaining how exactly 'true exteriority is in this gaze which forbids me my conquest.' In other words, the onus is on Levinas to explain the precise sense in which the face of the Other can invert the Sartrean dialectic of freedom, that is, explain why, in facing the Other, 'the structure of my freedom is … completely reversed.'[17]

Face 6
Face and Resistance

The eye is used to grasping. Green light, red light. A plane in the sky. Shoes in a shop window. The bored clerk. The cop waving hands. A car reversing. The street is blocked – roadwork (an orange sign). A homeless person sitting on an improvised armchair. A white cat looks down from the balcony. On the wall of the building across the street, a model posing, she's 20m high. The gaze frames the visible without leaving a trace of otherness. For Levinas, when the gaze directs itself forward, what you see is what there is – various kinds of more or less complex objects that are always already part of different relations with other objects, creating different states of affairs that are, again, characterized by different levels of complexity.

The doctor looks at an x-ray. The high-school senior watches a clip. The fan watches a basketball game. At the supermarket, the shopper's gaze glides over the shelves. The bouncer's gaze identifies who to let into the club. The gaze, according to Levinas, reproduces and perpetuates the rule of the object. It is the exemplary representative of the regime of the same. But precisely within the context of the same, at the very core of the measured frame within which the gaze operates in organizing the visual, an alternative possibility lies in wait. The other possibility is not of our making but is already open toward us, even if we have not yet seen or heard. How? In what way? It is there as a non-frontal dimension of the visual, a dimension that never takes the form of a 'given,' a passivity that lends itself to the holding of the eye.

At the heart of the frontal space of sense lies a diagonal, a fault line, a Great Rift Valley that creates a slant, an inclination that does not allow vision to give us, as is its habit, things as simply given. Where does this happen? In the face of the other person. Facing me, the Other's face hides an infinity that resists my gaze, refusing to be contained in what I see. In the encounter with the Other's face, my gaze fails to reduce distances, contrary to itself. Even when close, the face I see remains always at a distance, perhaps like the experience Sartre describes vis-à-vis Giacometti's sculptures. Furthermore, as the gaze draws closer and closes in on the face, as the gaze focuses and grasps the objective dimensions of the face, so a deeper and starker abyss opens up in the frame of reference it has built for itself. In the face turned toward me, the law of the object is breached, bringing about what Levinas understand as 'an overflowing of objectifying thought by a forgotten experience.'[1]

The face resists the rule of the gaze or, more precisely, the face is itself resistance. But this resistance is entirely unusual, one that does not close itself to the contemplating gaze. Contrary to a door closing in our face and hiding what is behind it, contrary to a hand stretching out to block the camera's field of vision, the face opposes the gaze openly, candidly, from within its nakedness. Levinas writes:

> There is first the very uprightness of the face, its upright exposure, without defense. The skin of the face is that which stays most naked, most destitute. It is the most naked, though with a decent nudity. It is the most destitute also: there is an essential poverty in the face; the proof of this is that one tries to mask this poverty by putting on poses, by taking on a countenance.[2]

Levinas ties the 'essential poverty' of the face to its extreme exposure, to the fact that its appearance invariably gives it away, does not allow it to hide. Even when 'putting on a face,' the face is still there, always entirely in the open, as if outside itself, without disguise or cover. The face, even when displaying maximal restraint, control, or self-containment is essentially exposed, vulnerable. Its vulnerability is not relative. The human face, the face in its humanity, is the epitome of vulnerability. Unlike the animal, whose vulnerability is denoted by the wound, the blemish, the piercing howl, human vulnerability comes to the fore in the face's range of expressivity: a lost, panicked, scared, desperate, humiliated, imploring face, but also no less the happy, relishing, dreaming face – 'the humanity of man – is a rupture of being.'[3]

And yet, despite its vulnerability – and perhaps due to it – 'there is a commandment in the appearance of the face, as if a master spoke to me.'[4] The weakness of the face, then, is also the source of its strength. Levinas describes this as follows:

> Here is established a relationship not with a very great resistance, but with the absolutely other, with the resistance of what has no resistance, with ethical resistance. It opens the very dimension of infinity, of what puts a stop to the irresistible imperialism of the same and the I. We call a *face* the epiphany of what can thus present itself directly, and therefore also exteriorly, to an I.[5]

The face of the other person appears in its opposition to the schematic nature of consciousness, to the hegemony of the ego. In the presence of the Other, the ego cannot proceed as usual, conducting itself as the centre of the world. The term 'cannot' is elusive. In the usual understanding of the word, the ego *can* definitely continue in its ways, just as the hurrying SUV driver *can* ignore the fact that a dog is by the side of the road or that a child is trying to cross – he *can* be heavy-handed and go on. But in another sense, the ego also *cannot* do this: 'cannot' in the sense that its ability, its power, encounters a 'Not' that appears precisely because it indeed can. Like the face, the ethical command is vulnerable. Not only *can* this command be breached, but the very background for its emergence is the possibility and the inclination to breach it.

The face has no frontal power. It has no tanks, clubs, or enforcement forces. Indeed, the face cannot stop the 'imperialism of the same and the I,' but it can stand up to it as a subversive cell opposes a tyrannical regime. The resistance of the face is manifest in the new horizon it creates for the ego's space of conduct. The conduct in the presence of the Other's face opens up the non-trivial sense of 'you cannot': an unenforceable obligation, a command that can always be breached, the ethical imperative. Beyond the possible admonishment for one or another action, the Other's face is already, at all times, evidence of my excessive power. As the face appears, a trajectory shows itself in the space of the ego, one that can be effaced but not erased: a trajectory of extreme alterity, of an external presence that in essence does not belong and will always remain foreign to the horizons of meaning that define the world of the I. When meeting

> the total uncoveredness and nakedness of his defenseless eyes ... the solipsist disquietude of consciousness ... comes to an end: true exteriority is in this gaze which forbids me my conquest. Not that conquest is beyond my too weak powers, but I *am no longer able to have power*: the structure of my freedom is ... completely reversed.[6]

The face of the Other 'reverses' the freedom structure of the self, a structure growing from the solipsistic life that consciousness has adopted for itself. The face reveals that the autonomy of the self is preceded by heteronomy. In the presence of the Other's face, the I directly experiences the existence of an exteriority that causes it to lose its standing as the sole centre of its world: a fundamental setting is thus destabilized but, at the same time, something fundamental reveals itself. The self encounters a non-trivial fact: it is not alone. It is not alone, but not only in the trivial factual sense that there are other people around, that someone is going up with you in the elevator, that there are other people in the movie hall, in the street, in the house. The crafty politician, for instance, and certainly the corrupt one, knows all too well that there are other people around. His conduct – and the measure of his success – is entirely dependent on his ability to anticipate and take into account other people's reactions, on the power to manipulate people. In a different context, the cautious driver also takes into account the existence and the behaviour of other people. But this is not what is at stake here. Both the politician and the cautious driver relate to the existence of other people as objective facts that one must learn and contend with. Their attitude to the Other does indeed leave room for a multiplicity of other subjects, but only from a perspective where the self remains its absolute and unquestionable centre. This is precisely the solipsistic stance that Levinas speaks of: solus ipse – a position that cannot uphold itself in the self's encounter with the face.

In its desires, intentions, plans, the I is constantly moving toward the objects that populate its world, always in a dynamic of relationships with these objects, which are already part of its immersion practices of usage and consumption that allow it to realize itself in the world. The encounter with the Other's face creates an interruption in this forward movement, generating a movement in the opposite direction – a movement toward the self, one that turns the I into its object.

One familiar example of this kind of movement is shame, which grows when we discover ourselves reflected in the Other's gaze. Sartre understands shame as paradigmatic of the self's existence vis-à-vis the Other – a theme that Levinas takes up while reformulating its meaning. For Sartre, '*Shame* is by nature recognition. I recognize that I am as the Other sees me,'[7] and, in that sense, shame is an essential failure of my freedom to be who I want to be. Shame thus attests to the self's recognition that it is an object for the Other and, more generally, that it is enslaved to an ontology whose principle of action is the oppressive dialectic of the gaze. By contrast, Levinas is willing to accept neither a dialectic nor a struggle between opposing forces. The Other 'does not stop me like a force blocking my force'[8] and more generally 'does not limit the freedom of the same.'[9]

According to Levinas, shame is not related to any specific act or event but follows from a fundamental discovery of the ego about itself. This is a '*shame* freedom has of itself, discovering itself to be murderous and usurpatory in its very exercise.'[10] As with Sartre, Levinasian shame grows out of the internalization of a fundamental problem concerning the freedom structure of the self. Contrary to Sartre, however, shame is not a recognition of the ultimate impasse, the necessary failure of the intersubjective condition; rather, it constitutes a new starting point. In this respect, it is more similar to Alcibiades' shame that, as we hear in Plato's *Symposium*, is aroused by the presence of Socrates and leads Alcibiades to a new self-understanding and to the possibility of becoming a better person. Yet, whereas for Plato the reflective dimension of shame is created through the encounter with oneself in the 'mirror' set by the Other (Socrates), Levinas refuses, as noted, to locate shame within the symmetrical structure of reflection and mirroring. The face of the Other does not set a mirror to the ego but creates instead a microscopical interruption in the courses of the I's conduct, one that 'puts into question the naïve right of my powers, my glorious spontaneity as a living being, a "force on the move."'[11]

The interruption that the Other's face creates in the spontaneous movement of the self does not originate in the face's capacity to defeat the Other's will to power, or in its ability to explain to the self something about itself. Rather, it results from the manner in which, at the core of the self's space of action, the face instils a dimension of sense that the self can neither frame nor contain. As such, the face is a spoke in the wheel, not allowing the self to take the closed and unified structure of its world as self-evident or as natural. To put this in terms borrowed from a completely different lexicon: Tony Soprano too has panic attacks; indeed, the entire plot of *The Sopranos* revolves around this panic. At the same time, however, what concerns us here is not the existential angst that swamps the self facing its finitude or the meaninglessness of existence but another kind of anxiety, one that is ethical at heart and that clearly articulates itself in the question: 'What have I done?!'

For Levinas, the structure of a question is fundamental to the description of the self's standing vis-à-vis the face of the Other. In the presence of this face, the ego finds itself called into question. This is a theme that recurs in Levinas: the infinite that is revealed in the face 'puts into question' not only 'the naïve right of my powers,' but, as noted, 'my glorious spontaneity as a living being.' 'We name this calling into question of my spontaneity by the presence of the Other, ethics,'[12] or, elsewhere, 'the calling in question of the I, coextensive with the manifestation of the Other in the face, we call language.'[13] We will have to explain how the phenomenon of language enters this picture, but let us first concentrate on explaining the question that the ego encounters in the presence of the Other's face: What does it mean to be called into question?

The structure of being called into question involves several elements. First, it presupposes a somewhat uncharted passivity whose 'other,' active side, is far more familiar to us. Turning to our everyday experience, we find it easier to reconstruct the act of questioning or of casting doubt on something. In calling something into question, we retreat from our (explicit or implicit) agreement to accept that thing or condition as self-evident and demand that it be re-examined and reconsidered. In facing the Other, the ego is the one finding itself as an object of a question, the focus of an uncertain situation whose status is pending. Like Sartre, here too, the face of the Other clearly attests to the self's existence as an object. But whereas for Sartre the Other is the one who pronounces my verdict, facing the Other for Levinas more closely resembles awaiting a verdict, always pending though never enforceable.

Whereas for Sartre, then, the Other's gaze determines the self's tragic fixation as object, for Levinas it opens up a possibility of rescue, that is, of liberating the self from the traditional structure of the subject. What one discovers when finding oneself in the position of an object, of a question, is not a closed structure that locks up the self's original openness but, on the contrary, a possible opening in the self's rigid and fixating structure. In the presence of the Other's face, the self's status as the *subject* of its own life plot is no longer obvious. The self can no longer be 'posited as the "indeclinable nominative: assured of its own right to be," but recovers itself through "the timidity of the non-intentional ... [a] passivity from start," and the accusative in a sense its first "case."'[14] The self's encounter with the face opens up the question of the self as subject. The subject becomes a question.

The self is accustomed to its role as a subject, a role that, for Levinas, is never simply given. The assumption of this role depends on several preconditions whose existence the self finds convenient, and perhaps even important, to forget. These conditions pertain to the constant maintenance of its identity and unity. Being a self, according to Levinas, is a non-trivial project contingent on the human ability to forge and stabilize, within the river of time and change, a distinctive structure with a determinate form of appearance. The self is an achievement of a consciousness that succeeded in finding means for suspending reality's immediate and direct weight, thereby creating for itself a private intimate space from which it can go out into the world and to which it can withdraw in return. Setting up and preserving this domestic space is not an easy task, but it is usually attained to the satisfaction of consciousness, which manages to filter and organize reality to fulfil its domestic requirements and even its needs for expansion and control. 'And here every power begins,' says Levinas, in a passage with Nietzschean overtones.

> The surrender of exterior things to human freedom through their generality does not only mean, in all innocence, their comprehension, but also their being taken in hand, their domestication, their possession. Only in possession does the I complete the identification of the diverse.[15]

In order to stabilize the identity structure of the self, consciousness must level the heterogeneity and strangeness of reality, submit everything to a standard that allows the ego domination and control.

In it is dissolved the other's *alterity*. The foreign being, instead of maintaining itself in the inexpugnable fortress of its singularity, becomes a theme and an object ... It falls into the network of a priori ideas ... so as to capture it.[16]

This is how, according to Levinas, cognitively oriented consciousness promotes 'the conquest of being.'[17]

But if things do not resist the ruses of thought, and confirm the philosophy of the same, without ever putting into question the freedom of the I, is this also true of men? Are they given to me as the things are? Do they not put into question my freedom?[18]

Levinas, as noted, answers this question in the affirmative. Unlike objects, humans create turmoil in the movement of the self, a spin that places the self at the centre of a question that is not only posed to it but of which it is also the subject. The subject of the question is the self and the form of this question, should we try to articulate it, is: 'You?' or 'Are you?'

Questions typically operate in a mode antithetical to that of a fact-depicting statement, an assertion expressing a proposition that determines the state of things: 'The general form of propositions is: This is how things are.'[19] The sentence tells us that the situation is this-and-that, and it does so by connecting, weaving, subordinating the subject of the sentence (usually some object in the world) to a predicate (some feature, state or action of the object): 'The man – is going down the stairs,' 'the window – is illuminated,' 'two crows – are on the roof of the car.' In characterizing the man as going down the stairs, or the window *as* illuminated, the sentence offers us meaning.

In contrast, a question is what unties the inner linking through which a statement conveys meaning. *Is* the window illuminated? The question does not eliminate the possibility expressed in the sentence but only brackets the statement's assertive force. The question enables the sentence to retain its sense without granting necessity or validity to what is expressed. The question neutralizes the assertive power of the sentence, its judgment structure or verdict-like quality. Whereas the fact-depicting sentence is a linguistic structure that closes and determines the meaning of things as this-and-that, the question functions as a vector that reopens the configuration of sense that has crystallized before us. Thus, while the ego routinely bases its conduct on an assertive principle of action that sanctifies its self-identity and its ownership of the surrounding world, the encounter with the Other fractures the cohesiveness of this structure of sense. Meeting a face, the ego finds itself in the proximity of what it can neither seize nor own, of what consciousness can neither frame nor ever 'bring back' home: consciousness thus encounters what prevents it from carrying on the movement to which it is so used to – one of closing a circle, of self-assertion and self-determination.

> A face imposes itself upon me without my being able to be deaf to its call or to forget it … Consciousness loses its first place. The presence of a face thus signifies an irrecusable order, a command, which puts a stop to the availability of consciousness. Consciousness is called into question by a face … A face confounds the intentionality that aims at it.[20]

The presence of the face undermines the self-confidence of consciousness. In a police investigation, the accusing finger also has a destabilizing effect. But whereas this effect reflects a potential or actual threat, linked to our acquaintance with police power and police brutality and the fear they evoke, the face that concerns Levinas lacks any such power. Its form of encounter is pacifist. The resistance of the face to the self's meaning-practices and consumption-routines has only a feeble, soundless, resonance, perhaps like the silence of the humiliated, or that of a dead butterfly in a child's hand, or of Cain over the body of his dead brother in the field, 'I didn't realize that you … I didn't realize that I …' Levinas writes:

I cannot evade the face of the other, naked and without resources. The nakedness of someone forsaken shown in the cracks in the mask of the personage, or in his wrinkled skin; his being 'without resources' has to be heard like cries not voiced or thematized, already addressed to God. There the resonance of silence – *Gelaut der Stille* – certainly sounds.[21]

Yet being called into question by the Other's face is a condition that has another significant aspect: it summons an answer. In the presence of the question that the face opens up, the self is compelled to respond. Not only does the face of the Other cast doubt on the egoistic structure of selfhood, but it also opens up to the self the possibility of an answer. How can the self respond to the face's demand for an answer? What can an answer to the question 'You?' mean? For Levinas, the inner form of a response is intimately entwined with that of responsibility. 'Positively, we will say that since the Other looks at me, I am responsible for him.'[22] Torn from its centre of gravity by the proximity of the Other, the self discovers responsibility as essential to its subjectivity: responsibility is not an external addition to the kernel of selfhood, but selfhood itself already rests on the depth structure of responsibility.

> The I loses its sovereign self-coincidence, its identification, in which consciousness returns triumphantly to itself to rest on itself. Before the exigency of the other the I is expelled from this rest ... But the calling into question of this wild and naive freedom for itself, sure of its refuge in itself, is not reducible to a negative movement ... The epiphany of the absolutely other is a face, in which the other calls on me and signifies an order to me through his nudity, his denuding. His presence is a summons to answer. The I does not only become aware of this necessity to answer, as though it were an obligation or a duty about which it would have come to a decision; it is in its very position wholly a responsibility ... To be an I means then not to be able to escape responsibility ...[23]

Thus, perhaps surprisingly, the Other's face also creates a place for the affirmation and validation of the self. In the presence of the face, the self discovers the ethical structure of its existence. The responsibility that discovers itself 'confirms the uniqueness of the I. The uniqueness of the I is the fact that no one can answer for me.'[24] In the presence of the Other's face, the I finds itself compelled to respond to a question of which he or she are at the centre. But the answer to the question 'You?' is never theoretical. It is found in the very act of responding. Obviously, it is possible not to respond to the question, it is possible to avoid it, but whoever does attempt to answer is already saying: 'Here I am!' The answer 'Here I am' attests to the acceptance of the self's unity and uniqueness as resulting from the fact that 'no one can answer for me.'[25]

Face 7
Outside

1:30 AM at the computer
one more thing to prepare for tomorrow suddenly
in the thick air, coming from outside, crossing the threshold of
the window, a woman's voice, the ring of the table lamp spins.
One scream, then a pause and a fall in the frequency, like crying. A cut
that does not heal. Between her breaths, I hear the flat and prolonged
groan of a man. I get up from the chair and go to the window. The
woman lives on the ground floor. Light flickers through the narrow
window; I see the corner of a table, a cup, an ashtray, and perhaps
also a shadow moving across the painted, old Tel Aviv floor tiles. I
don't know her but it appears we are neighbours. Maybe I stood next
to her at the grocers or in line at the post office. Does that touch her
now? Does she love the man lying on top of her? (Am I wrong about
the roles here?) How much rent does she pay? The voice I hear is not
happy. It has no self-respect but does have, beyond any biography,
an impressive record. A motorcycle goes past. A neighbour closes a
kitchen cupboard. The man gets dressed. I know that he will leave
the building now. The entrance door slams. Why doesn't he stay? And
there is also the other question, more elusive, vague – the voice I heard
and that now
is heard no longer – this unpaved, pre-urban,
screenless, non-text, non-digital, non-cellular, stripped of
architecture, devoid of rationale, who does it call to
beyond the asphalt of the soul?

I don't know her. I don't know what she looks like. I don't know what she looks like – means, first of all, that I have not seen her face and, even if I have, I cannot identify it as hers. In Hebrew, face, *panim*, is plural. It is also both feminine and masculine. Perhaps, in the afternoon, I will take down the trash and she too will throw something into the green trash container shared by the two buildings. Together, but I will not recognize her face. Who is she? Today the question is still open, by tomorrow it will be erased.

Talk

Talk 1
The Face of Language

Face and discourse are tied. The face speaks. It speaks, it is in
this that it renders possible and begins all discourse.
Ethics and Infinity

The face is the vanishing point of the visual. Like the Cheshire Cat
in *Alice in Wonderland*, as the gaze concentrates on the face, so the
face fades away. What it leaves, according to Levinas, is an opening
whose boundlessness bewilders the orientation of the gaze; the
gaze loses its way, and its values and priorities are overturned.
This condition of the eye is, according to Levinas, the cradle of
speaking. As a turning, a *peniyya*, the face is the beginning of
speech. Levinas is saying that the seed from which meaning grows
lies in the manner that the Other turns toward me. This is not
a trivial claim and, indeed, it differs radically from paradigmatic
ways of accounting for the emergence of meaning in language.

Language, like the eye, is commonly understood in terms of its
ability to frame meanings: 'it's cloudy today,' 'tomorrow it will clear.'
The emergence of meaning in language, then, is generally perceived
as following from language's inherent ability to represent, to frame,
different segments of the space of configurations of things. Meaning,
accordingly, is that which appears in the frame: content. Contents
are meanings structured as closed, self-sufficient objects packaged in
a manner that adequately fits the ability of consciousness to take in
and contain. Thus, for instance, in the online edition of a daily paper,
the following contents appear: 'Police say Prime Minister's testimony
will determine indictment on bank affair'; 'Senior official at the
Ministry of Health: We speculate in patients' rights'; 'Peres' plan will
not be implemented'; 'The IDF killed an unarmed Palestinian close

to the security fence.' These statements carry different meanings and signify different things, but they all share the same basic uniformity, a meaning structure that could be taken in and contained by you just as by anyone else because it is never meant only for you, but always for everyone or for no one in particular. News announcements are contents that appear like packaged products on the shelf and, in this sense, their structure in no way differs from the ads scattered among them: 'National Lottery: Devotedly contributing to the community for 55 years,' or 'New! The bank brings Europe's stock markets into your living room.'

For Levinas, 'to reduce a reality to its content thought is to reduce it to the same … The most ponderous reality envisaged as an object of thought is engendered in the gratuitous spontaneity of a thought that thinks it.'[1] Under the sign of the same, the experience of meaning is homogeneously levelled, allowing meanings to emerge only through the established uniform pattern of framed contents. Is the conversation going on between us now, however, necessarily of this same kind? Yes and no. As a bearer of content, our talk indeed has a frontal dimension to it but, in analogy to the face, our talking also always involves a dimension that cannot be located on the map of the same, a reverberation of alterity that cannot be framed as content. The presence of the non-frontal is not 'something' that we can consume, and therefore remains foreign within our routines of meaning consumption. It is indeed concealed, just as when one orders a product online, it is so easy to forget the presence of human hands and the labour of people living in other places and under different conditions without whom this product would have been unavailable.

It is all too often difficult for us to acknowledge the non-frontal dimension of language, just as it is hard to hear sadness in a funny joke or longing in a sarcastic remark. But in recalling the unframed, one could for example make the point that, developmentally, this open space awakens long before things have content, before meanings are packed and presented as objects for consumption.

Similarly, we may recall how meaningful and alive the space of communication that opens up in the company of a baby can be. We spin webs of meaning, we connect – we touch, make sounds, movements, faces – without necessarily communicating any specific content. In adult life, when the object becomes dominant, it is usually difficult to discern the extent to which expression is always already lurking at the basis of our signification routines. But this dimension of language may at times surge as, for example, in the discourse of lovers, when the things that are talked about – the things said – matter less than the inner pulse, the very occurrence of talk from which determined meanings are born.

Equipped with these phenomenological insights, Levinas recognizes in the fully determined world of sense a dimension that the framing gaze, by its very nature, cannot contain: the emergence or becoming of the meaningful. Like Merleau-Ponty, Levinas is troubled by the failure of objective thought to make room for the ways in which the event of language comes into being. Framing language as a kind of object, however complex, precludes the possibility of seeing the very event of language or of experiencing language as an event because, when framed in this way, language can only appear as a fait accompli, as atemporal or, at least, as that whose temporality is a matter of the past. Levinas, like Merleau-Ponty, opposes the prevalent tendency to identify the essence of language with the cognitive, abstract structures that can be extracted from it. He writes: 'Signification is not an ideal essence or a relation open to intellectual intuition ... meaning is not produced as an ideal essence; it is said and taught by presence.'[2] Linguistic meaning does not stem from the 'I think' but from the living, embodied subject – the 'I can.'[3]

Yet, while explicitly concerned with the ways in which the living subject imbues language with meaning, the focus of Levinas' investigation clearly differs from that of Merleau-Ponty: what matters to Levinas is not the self and the character of its linguistic ties with the surrounding world, but how the other person appears in language and opens up a distance vis-à-vis the self. What is unique to Levinas' stance, then, is not only the importance he ascribes to the concreteness of the realm of sense but the very emphasis he places on the concrete presence of the Other in the self's space of language. 'Signification,' as noted,

> is not an ideal essence or a relation open to intellectual intuition. Instead, it is preeminently the presence of exteriority ... an original relation with exterior being ... it is a presence more direct than visible manifestation, and at the same time a remote presence – that of the Other.[4]

The analogy to the face is clear here: 'In the face, the expressed *attends* its expression ... in its own way it resists identification, does not enter into the already known, brings aid to itself ... speaks.'[5] The event of language is the Other's irruption into the cohesive identity of the self. Consequently, the possibility of meaning is what grows from the unlocking, the opening up of that identity structure to the foreign presence of the Other.

From another perspective, the event of language – talk – is never a neutral event where the self can ostensibly remain an external listener, a distant spectator. In speaking, the I is being addressed and, as such, is exposed to that turning made by a speaker, that is, by a person entering the field of spoken language from an elsewhere, one who 'expresses its very expression, [and] always remains master of the meaning it delivers.'[6] In speaking, the self is exposed to 'the presence of exteriority,' a presence that, despite all possible intimacy, will, in essence, necessarily remain foreign. Hence, since 'the presence of exteriority' is always part of the unfolding of meaning, signification is never exhaustible by the contents, the ideal essences signified in a manner befitting the structure of thought. Whereas meaningful talk always depends on a movement of framing and presenting contents (that is, a movement in the sphere of the same), it also consists of an opposite trajectory, a perpetual unravelling of the homogeneous fabric woven by the common signification of words.

Spoken language rests on the saying of things, but the saying itself is not identical to the things said nor can it be understood through them. In Levinas' later writing, this distinction between the Saying (*le dire*) and the Said (*le dit*) becomes crucial. On the one hand, language opens up to meaning through a movement of alterity that breaks through the borders of the self; on the other, language can only become significant through the apparent closure of sense, the framing and determination of shared contents that are located nowhere in particular and are equally accessible to all. Contrary to the Said, the roots of the saying are found in the real, living relationship that bears – that sustains – the linguistic event. The Saying grows out of the speakers' singular presence, out of a possibility of a proximity pervaded by the irreducible distance between self and Other. In this sense, the 'proximity beyond intentionality,'[7] a 'proximity antecedent to any convention'[8] that Levinas describes as 'a language without words or propositions, [as] pure communication,'[9] is not only different from and even contrary to the Said but indeed disappears, devoured by the Said. The Saying goes underground when we listen to language only through the contents it represents or through the effects it creates, that is, when our relation to meaning is frontal. 'The saying, that is, the face, is the discretion of an unheard-of proposition, an insinuation, immediately reduced to nothing.'[10]

The question that emerges here is how to think about language without depriving it of its vitality. Talk is unique in that it opens up for language the possibility of transcending beyond the replicating domain of empty clichés, not only in the less common contexts such as poetry, for example, but precisely in the most standard configurations of sense available to us. Attentive to the inner pulse of the life of sense, Levinas recognizes an irregular beat resonating with the unresolved presence of the Other. For him, this is precisely what enables us to say 'Hi, how are you?' or 'thank you so much' in a way that is not merely an echo or a quotation of something that was already said somewhere else by someone else. How does our speaking open up to meaning? The inception of meaning is found neither in language's (depictive) relation to the specific thing that is spoken of nor in the particularity of the linguistic act that we perform in speaking. Instead, talk can become meaningful because of the manner in which it is tied to – our standing vis-à-vis the face of – the Other.

Poet Yehuda Amichai writes: 'And death is when someone keeps calling you/and calling you/ and you no longer turn around to see/ who it is.'[11] Similarly, a speaking wherein 'you no longer turn to see who it is' is dead-talk, a language of tombstones. In this respect, when Levinas claims that 'the face ... renders possible and begins all discourse,' I take him to be referring to that constitutive turn (*peniyya*) that brings language to life, a facing in relation to which our speaking always takes the form of a response – a responsibility – toward what can never become our own. Listening to the non-frontal dimension of language, then, depends on our ability to lend an ear to the resonance of an impenetrable depth found in our words. This inaccessible depth is the place of entry into the language of the other person, one whose words I may grasp and command but whose inner connection to language shall remain closed off for me. Talk never takes place 'there,' in front of us, nor does it make room for speakers who, as in a PlayStation game, could in principle be just anyone. To speak always implies a condition of being trapped, whose other side is being elicited by the presence of a singular and irreplaceable Other. As such, speaking always takes the form of an response to *a you*, an answer – a *teshuvah* that in Hebrew, as Levinas knew well, also means 'repentance' – to the question posed to the self by the very presence of the Other: 'The calling in question of the I, coextensive with the manifestation of the Other in the face, we call language.'[12] What Levinas thus illuminates is the presence of language's human face. Language has a face, and its call for us to listen depends on our ability to see its face.

Talk 2
Expression

The first question has to be: can discourse
signify otherwise than by signifying a theme?

God and Philosophy

Levinas' phenomenology of the face involves two levels of insight.
One, as noted, concerns the distinctiveness and uniqueness of
the face (in relation to the object), while the other deals (again,
vis-à-vis the object) with the primacy of the face as an origin of
meaning. In this context, Levinas recurrently makes the claim
that beyond the unique character of the face's appearance, the face
provides a more original archetype of sense, one that allows objects
to bear a meaning in the first place. The key distinction for Levinas
here is that between 'representation' and 'expression.' Whereas the
represented object always appears to consciousness as a closed and
complete form of meaning (i.e. as content), the face appears as
that which expresses itself: in self-expression, the face addresses
consciousness as that which ceaselessly transcends any given form.

Levinas writes: 'A face is not like a plastic form, which is always
already deserted, betrayed, by the being it reveals, such as marble
from which the gods it manifests already absent themselves ...
In a face the expressed *attends* its expression, expresses its very
expression.'[1] Unlike the statue or the masque, or indeed, unlike the
meaning-bearing object, the face opens itself up to meaning without
being subject to a particular 'plastic form' or to the connection of
this form to the context where it acquires its meaning. Contrary
to the statue, the face represents nothing; contrary to the object, it
serves nothing: the face is in the world, but is not part of that large
storage space of existing things. It has no role to play, and yet it is

91

actively present through the unceasing movement it generates from within itself toward the outside.

This movement, which can be understood neither in terms of representation nor of functionality, is what Levinas calls 'expression.' Expression is indeed connected to the giving of form, but is not an externalization or a signification of any hidden content. 'Expression does not consist in *giving* us the Other's interiority.'[2] Unlike the mask, the face is neither a screen nor a façade hiding a more genuine or vital dimension of the other person. It is itself a revelation of life, a self-revelation. The face has depth, but its depth is not part of some additional space behind it. The face is the infinitely thin surface of expression, of what unfolds and flows on its own accord, originating from a source that, surprisingly, is not separate from the flow but rather constantly present within it. Levinas characterizes expression as follows:

> Expression is not produced as the manifestation of an intelligible form that would connect terms to one another so as to establish, across distance, the assemblage of parts in a totality, in which the terms joined up already derive their meaning from the situation created by their community ... This 'circle of understanding' is not the primordial event of the logic of being. Expression precedes these coordinating effects visible to a third party.[3]

Expression, according to Levinas, is not a synthetic form. It bears meaning, but its meaningfulness is not dependent on the external connection between terms that, like the noun and the verb, create a structure of signification. In a world ruled by the same, meaning typically appears as a thing among others, as an object, a frame of content. Content is nothing but the contained; what is always already framed, and what is framed is a determinative connection between terms, one that allows something to show itself *as* something (for example the glass, as full) and enables us to understand what shows itself as 'this and that' (to see that the glass is full, to say 'the glass is full'). But expression, as Levinas argues, is not part of the circle of signification and understanding. It is more primary in that it consists of an opening of precisely what signification closes up. Expression opens up a possibility that precedes its realization as a 'this and that,' a movement that precedes the state of stillness wherein the object of understanding is found. The face's existence is thus essentially expressive: the face is expression before it expresses anything in particular. In being expressive, the face is present in a way that precedes its appearance as tired, sad, tense, happy and so forth—it is present prior to the crystallization of that pattern of signification so central and familiar to us from the everyday experience, prior to the thing. The face is originally a prologue, a pre-face.

Yet, the primacy of the face that concerns Levinas is not (only) that of the pre-thematic over the thematically determined, of the experiential over the conceptual. Levinas does not focus on the temporal precedence of expression, or on its precedence in the sense of being an (undetermined) substratum from which determinate forms can emerge. Levinas writes: 'In a face the expressed *attends* its expression, expresses its very expression.' What matters to him is that an organizing presence shows itself in the face, which is essentially different from the one that creates the structure of the object. What 'holds' and 'is held' in the movement of the face is not the 'what' but the 'who.' The who is not a specific kind of a what, it is not *there* as a some-thing, and, as such, it is also never simply given to – never a given of – a perceiving consciousness. The relation of the who to the I is never frontal. Rather, it always shows itself within an already occurring movement toward the I, one that cuts the distance between us, encroaching on the I's private sphere (in Levinas' later works, this movement of encroachment is radicalized and the I is presented as persecuted by the Other).

The face, then, is not only the site of the visible's emergence from the invisible but also the movement of the Other's constant entry into the realm of the same: the face is above all a turn, a turning from you toward me – always in the singular. This also explains the primacy of expression: as a turning toward, expression for Levinas is a unique movement of the becoming of sense that precedes general given forms of signification and that, furthermore, grounds the very possibility of such forms. What concerns Levinas is the vector operative in enabling the thing to emerge as meaningful in the space between you and I, opening up a possibility of understanding what shows itself and speaking to one another about it.

'Face and discourse are tied. The face speaks. It speaks, it is in this that it renders possible and begins all discourse.' The face is the distant and inaccessible end of the field of vision, but also the threshold of, the gate to the field of language. As Levinas argues, however, the opening of the face to discourse – expression – does not show itself easily to every gaze. 'Expression precedes these coordinating effects visible to a third party.' That is, whereas the products of sense (e.g. the contents of a speech act) are generally accessible beyond the actuality of a dialogical situation – I can be updated on, and understand, the things you said in a conversation in which I was not present – the primacy of expression has no place and is in fact erased when framed by an external 'third party.' That is, there is no access to the dimension of expression for one who is not already part of the conversation. And in this respect, the primacy of expression can reveal itself to me, only when I respond to the actual turning by which your words bear themselves toward me.

Talk 3
The First Word

Meaning is the face of the Other, and all
recourse to words takes place already with the
primordial face to face of language.

Totality and Infinity

What Levinas offers is a form of sensibility, a mode of looking, a perspective from which the unfolding of sense can be seen in a different manner. What he offers is a non-canonical optics, one that is attentive to the danger of reproducing the common structure dominating the appearance of meaning, an optics intended to allow us to view the domain of sense in a non-frontal manner, as a face: 'meaning is the face of the Other.' Levinas teaches us how to see the Other as an integral part of the very givenness of sense; that is, to see or recognize that the meaningful originates in a linking – a relationship – that neither belongs nor can be subordinated to the cognitive structure of subject-object.

According to Levinas, the frontal relationship between subject and object is not, in itself, sufficient for sustaining meaningfulness. The space of correlation between subject and object lacks the kind of oxygen needed for the sustenance of meaning. It is devoid of any dimension of alterity and consists solely of reproductions (and reproductions of reproductions) of the principle of the same. The mirror game of the same cannot engender meaning; it is barren because it is essentially confined to, and can never transcend, its limits. For Levinas, however, the phenomenon of meaning can unfold only in the opening up of the same to a dimension of alterity. Rather than abstract, this opening is entirely concrete, and what generates it is the unresolved presence – the turning, the face – of the Other. The appearance of those forms of signification that

95

are caught, that begin and never cease to flicker between subject and object, between the eye and the screen or between the ear and the word, is made possible by a more primordial surge of meaning that already responds to the Other's presence.

The priority that concerns Levinas is primarily conceptual rather than temporal, but it can also be anchored in a temporal manner by attending to the formation and development of sense in the life of infants. Hence, by following Donald Winnicott's psychoanalytic analyses, for example, specific aspects of 'the birth of meaning' growing from the mother-baby relationship may be used to enrich the Levinasian metaphysical outlines. In this context, we may emphasize how the upholding of the I-world setting, with its various levels of significance, develops gradually within the space of the primary contact between mother and baby. This space enables and secures the development and crystallization of the same but also remains open to a dimension of alterity and, moreover, to the permanent tension between identity and alterity to which the baby is exposed through the mother's dual presence.[1] The primary appearance of meaning, then, is not an anonymous event (self-cohesion and presentation of something that happens *there, in front of the baby*), but a possibility revealed to the baby from within the horizons of its unique connection to a concrete alterity, to another person: usually, and first of all, its mother.

Similarly, in our 'mother tongue' we find ourselves within a familiar and intimate space of meaning because the mother's primary presence has succeeded in softening for us the strenuous encounter with a mute and arbitrary reality. Hence, the fact that the realm of sense opens itself up before us so 'naturally' does not only attest to the self's ability to adapt to the world and find meanings in it, but first of all to the human 'tenderness' that the self receives from outside, a tenderness that, to begin with, cushions its encounter with the world. In Levinas' terms, the familiarity of things assumes intimacy, and this intimacy, before attaching itself to any specific object, '*is intimacy with someone*'; furthermore, 'the primary hospitable welcome that describes the field of intimacy, is the Woman.'[2]

Hence, whereas our mother tongue does allow us to feel at home with the words and meanings common in our language, the space of intimacy that it creates is already touched by the presence of alterity, a presence that will always remain external and inaccessible to the speaking subject. Similarly, our words, according to Levinas, do not furnish us access to any given, self-subsistent, homogeneous domain of sense, but position us in the field of an event that is already invariably polarized by the presence of the Other. 'The essence of language,' writes Levinas, 'is in the relation with the Other,'[3] and in this sense, 'all recourse to words takes place already with the primordial face to face of language.'

The presence of the Other is a critical mass, a centre of gravity that irregularly modifies the space of meaning. This irregular, non-frontal relationship is, in Levinas' terms, the 'face to face.' And so, the 'recourse to words,' the movement of articulation, never takes place in a continuous and homogeneous space of neutral meanings lending themselves to representation. Rather, this movement always occurs in incoherent, discontinuous and intricate spaces – such as the *Marsyas* of Anish Kapoor – which do not allow the gaze to hold the significations of language at a fixed distance from the Other's speech. To phrase this differently, language is a non-Euclidean space. It has no coordinates that could define the relationship between our linguistic existence and that of the Other. As such, language provides neither a frame of commensurability nor a common denominator between the self and the Other. It is indeed a space where we encounter the Other, but this encounter has no grounding in the shared homogeneity of sense or in any identical kernel of signification. Instead, it is based on a relationship with an extreme foreignness that can never be domesticated.

In this respect, the fact that conversation partners can communicate and reach mutual understanding is often misleading, since it encourages us to assume that 'at the basis' of what is said is a sameness merely waiting to be discovered. According to Levinas, the opposite is the case: 'Language, source of all signification, is born in the vertigo of infinity, which takes hold before the straightforwardness of the face.'[4] Levinas does not hold that understanding is impossible, or that the sense of reciprocity created in the conversation is an illusion. He argues, rather, that the very possibility of mutual understanding develops from an undecipherable kernel of alterity, from an unassailable abyss. Even when language does enable us to understand one another, it never provides us with a consistent and uniform ground of sense but merely with ways of living with the gaping chasm that we generally prefer to avoid looking at directly. 'The vertigo of infinity' describes an important dimension of our experience with language, one that all too often we tend to ignore. We dull and obliterate its effect by clinging to the frontal side of language, to its contents – 'what you said' we insist 'is that things are such and such ...' – precisely because this vertigo is essential to our being with and being in language.

For Levinas, the possibility of recognizing the non-frontal side of sense is intimately linked to the possibility of encountering 'the straightforwardness of the face,' that is, of finding for ourselves a place, an orientation, within language that allows conversing face to face. In this sense, a conversation, in the full sense of the word, is that movement toward mutual understanding that neither conceals nor dismisses the presence of the abyss between self and Other but, on the contrary, confirms and validates its existence. This ability to 'see' or 'hear' the resonance of alterity in language is, however, elusive and entirely non-trivial; this mode of responsiveness has no recipe, and it is not clear where precisely to look, what to listen to, or what to hold on to in order to encounter it.

Talk 4
Saying and Betraying

A methodological problem emerges at the centre of Levinas' later conception of language, one that continues to preoccupy Levinas and is never resolved by him. Levinas writes:

> We have been seeking the otherwise than being from the beginning, and as soon as it is conveyed before us it is betrayed in the said that dominates the saying which states it. A methodological problem arises here, whether the pre-original element of saying ... can be led to betray itself by showing itself in a theme ... and whether this betrayal can be reduced: whether one can at the same time know and free the known of the marks which thematization leaves on it by subordinating it to ontology. Everything shows itself at the price of this betrayal, even the unsayable. In this betrayal the indiscretion with regard to the unsayable, which is probably the very task of philosophy, becomes possible.[1]

In order to call attention to the presence of a radical alterity within the space of language, Levinas draws, as suggested, a fundamental distinction between the 'Saying' and the 'Said.' Yet, in distinguishing between these two dimensions of the linguistic phenomenon, the very move that allegedly opens up for him the possibility of transcending the same also appears to close up this option. Whereas the saying, according to Levinas, harbours a transcendent dimension that cannot be conceptualized, language's basic structure of intelligibility inevitably 'dominates the saying which states it.' As a dimension *of* language, the Saying cannot manifest itself independently of language's essential cognitive structure and, therefore, the Said ultimately 'devours' and ultimately eliminates the Saying.

Language, by bearing content, enables us to share knowledge. Yet, content is precisely what obliterates the resonance of alterity since its mode of signification is uniform, self-sufficient and self-identical. For Levinas, content is a presentation of meaning that remains indifferent to the singularity and otherness of the speaking subject. It remains completely unaffected by the singular tongue, the breath, the voice that speaks. It is a barren modality of sense that cannot make any room for what Levinas understands as that infinitely distant proximity between self and Other, that 'proximity qua saying, contact, sincerity of exposure.'[2] And here is the 'betrayal' that concerns Levinas: the Saying cannot manifest itself in any meaningful way because it is inevitably nullified in the course of its linguistic expression. The Saying, then, finds itself betrayed because it can only show itself as what it is not: as a 'this and that,' as signification determined in and by its placement in a conceptual scheme, as a theme.

Structurally, this is not a new philosophical problem. Throughout its history, philosophy has acknowledged situations where its own language becomes a limitation, situations where the essence of philosophical language seems to prevent the expression of a philosopher's vision of transcendence. In this context, what singles out Levinas' stance is his insistence on articulating the problem of transcendence free from the horizons of ontological discourse. For Levinas, ontological language is a language whose movement and inner rhythm are regulated by its affinity to, by a quest for, a fit between thought and being. This language of essence and sameness is just as dominant, however, in philosophies where transcendence is fundamental. That is, according to Levinas, philosophical moves that explicitly make room for transcendence nevertheless typically remain captive in a framework that sanctifies the same and precludes alterity. This occurs because their attempt to transcend the ontological realm usually presupposes a conceptual opposition in which being (and thus the law of the same) can easily continue to echo through its negative reproduction:

> The philosopher finds language again in the abuses of language of the history of philosophy, in which the unsayable and what is beyond being are conveyed before us. But negativity, still correlative with being, will not be enough to signify the *other than being*.[3]

Consequently, for Levinas, the question of transcendence must be articulated 'otherwise than being from the beginning.' That is, it must be part of a radical attempt to set down the topography of a new question zone – a new discursive space – that will not allow the 'otherwise' and the 'beyond' to slide back into the realm of the thinkable. At the same time, Levinas avoids a frontal confrontation with ontology. He knows that negative or mirror pictures are no less problematic and his inquiry is therefore directed at the creation of a new topography based on the displacement of the paradigmatic role of being as origin, principle and centre of the meaningful.

Levinas wishes to replace the philosophical setting – the light, the clarity, the balance and the solidity – wherein the drama of being's disclosure traditionally unfolds. The alternative to which he commits himself is a philosophical space that, in principle, cannot uphold and contain itself because it is pervaded by the presence of an exteriority that resists integration. The space of thought breaks open and, contrary to its character, remains open to an unresolved presence that cannot be relegated to the neutral order of facts and is thereby experienced as an invasive and destabilizing event. This dimension of exteriority is what lurks in the enigma of the other person. The unresolved riddle, the Other's alterity, is the source of a 'pre-original element of saying' that exposes the ethical by consistently disrupting the ontological order.

Levinas writes, then, in an attempt to uncover a 'pre-original' dimension of language, one he identifies as conditioning the very possibility of discourse. And yet, in turning the notion of the saying into the Archimedean point of his thinking, Levinas finds himself facing a problem that he cannot easily solve or circumvent. Levinas recognizes that the relationship between the Said and the Saying cuts across philosophy's very possibility of talking about the saying in the first place: that is, any attempt to present the saying in philosophical language ultimately forces the Saying back into the context of the Said. Levinas acknowledges that his understanding of language bears directly on his own use of philosophical language and threatens, at least at first glance, to undermine the validity, the effectiveness and the truth of his own language. This problem is specifically intensified in the context of his unequivocal stance that the saying can never appear in its original form, since the said provides its essential structure of manifestation.

> But this pre-original saying does move into a language, in which saying and said are correlative of one another, and the saying is subordinated to its theme … The subordination of the saying to the said, to the linguistic system and to ontology, is the price than manifestation demands. In language qua said everything is conveyed before us, be it at the price of a betrayal.[4]

Levinas knows that to speak of the Saying without paying a price is impossible. The only question is what the price is and whether it can be paid without arriving at philosophical bankruptcy. 'Would not the bankruptcy of transcendence,' Levinas asks, 'be but that of a theology that thematizes the transcending in the logos, assigns a term to the passing of transcendence?'[5] Does Levinas' writing remain captive within the thematic order of the Said? Can the 'pre-original Saying' show itself in Levinas' philosophical language without being betrayed? Or, more generally, is philosophical language by its very nature a language of betrayal (as Levinas hints), or can it open up beyond the Said? 'How is the Saying, in its primordial enigma, said?' Levinas asks, 'how can transcendence withdraw from *esse* while being signalled in it?'⁶

Language Acts

There are different ways of answering these questions and Levinas appears to be giving one type of answer by engaging in the unique and experimental writing of *Otherwise than Being*. Even if the overall effect of this text is not clear-cut, Levinas' style of writing definitely conveys a sense of discomfort with the thematic structure of the Said and a refusal to cooperate with that hegemony. In this context, Levinas' commentators make a point of the manner in which Levinas' 'style of writing becomes increasingly sensitive to the problem of how the ethical saying is to be conceptualized' and suggest an understanding of *Otherwise than Being* as an attempt at – a gesture of – deconstruction: a writing that seeks to dismantle, to erode 'the limits of ontology and its claim to conceptual mastery, while also recognizing the unavoidability of the Said.'⁷ In a corollary manner, it is also suggested that *Otherwise than Being* should be read primarily as a 'performative enactment of an ethical writing,'⁸ that is, as a text whose contents are only the accompanying repercussions of its performative dimension.

In this reading, the central event of *Otherwise than Being* is not circumscribed by what the text says but by the very act of subverting the ontological in a manner that renders the ethical present. But are all possible disruptions of the ontological equal? Do they all evoke the ethical in the same way? Is the subversion of the ontological sufficient, in itself, for opening up of an ethical space? And, even if Levinas' writing does indeed challenge the hegemonic structure of the Said, is this challenge sufficient as an answer to the question of how – and whether – the Saying can be said at all? Can philosophy ultimately allow the saying to show itself or is betrayal part of the saying's unavoidable predicament?

Hence, when explaining Levinas' treatment of the Saying, scholarship on Levinas quite often refers to the distinction between the content and the act (or effect) of speech or, more generally, between the constative and the performative dimensions of language. This distinction grounds one of the central shifts in twentieth-century thought about language, one that accentuates the difference between language as describing a world and language as acting within the world. Rather than exhausting its essence, the power of language to represent a situation is only one of its broad gamut of functions, one of a range of ways wherein language is involved in creating and shaping the human condition. Being already 'in the world,' language is deeply connected to the domain of human action. Even before it says something specific, language is already permanently in action: it makes us remember and forget, it distorts, prompts, encourages, promises, asks, builds and destroys, sets rules, judges and permits.

Since Levinas is clearly preoccupied with language's possibility of signification beyond the said, the pragmatic dimension of language appears to be a natural and efficient candidate for locating the event of the Saying.[9] In my view, however, such an interpretation completely misses the point. Whereas Levinas clearly recognizes the centrality of the pragmatic dimension of discourse, he ultimately has no particular philosophical interest in this dimension (whose discovery he attributes to Heidegger) because for him, the pragmatic understanding of language can only reproduce the problems of the cognitive picture, albeit in the form of a – negative – mirror image. The framing of language in terms of its core content hides the transcendent presence of the interlocutor; but the focus on the action dimension of language does just the same since the speech act is intrinsically rule-governed, conventional and, as such, subordinate to the principle of the same.

Equating the saying with the act of language, then, is too simple a solution. If we could really get hold of the ethical dimension of language by splitting the linguistic phenomenon into its content and performative dimensions, wouldn't that completely deflate the methodological problem that so bothers Levinas? If the saying could be described and understood in terms of language's spectrum of action – one that is added to language's propositional or representational structure – this would subsume the Levinasian concept under the language of ontology and, in this respect, would largely mitigate its purported radicalism. Furthermore, when we try to explain the distinction between Saying and Said through the familiar set of oppositions used in the paradigmatic analysis of speech acts, we are inevitably buying into a dominant metaphysical picture of language that, in principle, cannot make room for the possibility of a transcendent alterity.[10]

In this respect, Levinas' move should be read as consisting in a dual liberation, releasing itself from two commonly accepted though opposite views of linguistic meaning: criticizing the understanding of linguistic meaning as a kind of logical possibility, while challenging the ostensibly opposite conception of meaning as primarily tied to the act of language: its force and effects.[11] Although these two approaches frame the linguistic event differently, both relate to the linguistic event as a kind of framable object, be it as content or as action. Both are held captive by the same 'frontal' gaze that remains blind to the incessant 'becoming' of language between us, between you and I – blind to the oblique movement of the Other's penetration into the realm of the same, a movement that sparks the possibility of discourse precisely because it breaks through the homogeneous, anonymous and familiar order of given linguistic possibilities.

Access

Given that the Saying is erased by the very form of its appearance (the Said), and that the Said is the essential form of language, is the encounter with the Other's alterity at all possible? Is alterity a dimension that can show itself and be heard in language? Is it possible for the transcendent to escape the essence that marks it? As a first step in answering these questions, we must recognize that they hide a conceptual pitfall, one that is hard to resist and into which even Levinas himself occasionally stumbles. The question of the possibility of the Saying's manifestation in language calls us to think of the saying within the horizons of a logical space that, in being what it is (i.e. logical) leaves no room for whatever lacks conceptual structure.

Therefore, if we reply to the question in its narrow sense, we must answer in the negative. But this negative response, which the question compels, does not attest to anything interesting or new, beyond the fact that the space of logical possibilities does not include what it cannot include by definition. Even if correct in a certain sense, the answer, like the question that provoked it, does not shed light on the phenomenon but actually closes off any insight we might have as to its concrete presence. If we find it impossible to encounter the Other's Saying, this is not because the Saying is missing in language, but rather because its turning toward us always precedes any encounter initiated by us. The Saying of the other person is always already there; its presence is concrete and conspicuous and does not depend on any form of logical assessment. Levinas is acquainted with the saying in a manner that is immediate and indisputable but not necessarily demonstrable conceptually. More accurately, the presence of the Saying is precisely what the philosopher cannot prove, deduce, or construe in any logical way, though he can at times help us become more responsive to that evasive presence. Here, the measure of a philosopher's pride or modesty is put to a test: a proud failure or a modest success.

The question of whether the Saying could be heard in language is not theoretical, at least not in the standard sense of the word. Instead, this question is inseparable from the very attempt to listen, an attempt whose success is related, in turn, to our position and orientation, as listeners, within the language we speak (the 'where are you?' question). And in order to listen, one must be careful not to succumb to several typical philosophical temptations. First, we must keep in mind that the saying is not a given but that its mode of givenness is unique and elusive. Its elusiveness is due not only to transcendence's unique structure of appearance, but also to its dependence on us as listeners and on our active positioning in its regard. The Saying is a real dimension of language but, despite its concreteness, it never presents itself to us as would, for example, a bowl of soup to a diner. The Saying is present, but it is never fully disclosed. It is not disclosed but neither is it concealed, as a jewel in a safe, or a letter in a locked drawer. So, how, in what way, is the saying both manifest and concealed? What matters here is not to hurry with an answer, to avoid adopting any ready-made well defined picture of the relationship between the uncovered and the concealed. This is precisely the meaning of being responsive to the Saying, what listening is about.

The understanding that, in language, the relationship between manifestation and concealment is never fully determined, liberates us from the expectation that the Saying should be given to experience as something immediate and simple. But this understanding also warns us against the opposite stance, which hurries to locate the saying beyond the limits of experience. Indeed, the saying is cancelled out, muted, by the language of the said. Again, however, we should not hasten to draw the general conclusion (one occasionally suggested by Levinas himself) that the language of thought is fundamentally incapable of echoing the saying. A conclusion of this type is one that takes for granted the antithetical character of the relationship between what belongs to the space of the said and what lies beyond it, construing this opposition around the idea of a clear boundary separating inside from outside.

The Saying calls for a suspension, perhaps a transcendence, of cognitive content, but we should also remember that, in itself, a non-conceptual or non-cognitive vision of language does not bring us any closer to the Saying. As we search for the Saying, identifying the delimiting effects of language's cognitive structure (the Said) is not enough. What we must do is overcome the temptation to totalize the prohibitive effect of language's limits, thereby avoiding the possibility that the protest against these limits might become another, possibly more dire, form of captivity. Interestingly, when one listens to another person, the structural limits of language become much less troubling. Or, more precisely, what is troubling in the encounter with these limits is not a general principle but barriers that are at times insurmountable though always concrete, barriers that only show themselves at the crossroads and the bifurcations of the specific conversations we have – with him, with her, with you.

Once we locate the (non-) concept of the Saying within the context of a living conversation with a specific Other, we may understand slightly better why Levinas insistently claims that the Saying grows from a tension that, for a thought reflecting on language from the outside, remains unresolved. The Saying does not require our conceptual, analytical, or logical reaffirmation. What the Saying awaits, rather, is attentiveness and further articulation of an intricate tension that marks the subliminal, mostly silent, currents through which radical transcendence can reside in the finite structures of spoken language.

How, then, can we respond to the echo, the buzz, or perhaps the stridency provoked by this tension without stifling it? Can we, in this context, learn a lesson from Kafka's parable about the philosopher seeking to understand the movement of a spinning top; the philosopher who, in his passion to understand the secret of this movement, grasps the top and examines it, stopping its movement and killing the event that had intrigued him? How can we think about the saying without halting its movement?

Phenomenology?

What seems to be called for is a phenomenology: a mode of thinking or a reflective attentiveness that focuses on the phenomenon while allowing it, in Heideggerian terms, to show itself from within itself. But can we speak of a phenomenology in the context of Levinas' later writings, and particularly in the context of *Otherwise than Being*? Does not the language of this text mark Levinas' final departure from phenomenology? In his later work, Levinas is openly ambivalent concerning the value of phenomenology. In itself, this ambivalence is not a new theme in Levinas. But whereas in *Totality and Infinity*, for example, his criticism of certain aspects of Husserl's phenomenology goes hand in hand with an explicit acknowledgment of his debt to Husserl and, moreover, together with the continual practicing of extensive phenomenological analyses, in *Otherwise than Being*, his critical view of phenomenology becomes unequivocal.

This criticism is driven by the work's distinctive shift toward a pure anti-phenomenological transcendence, in an explicit departure from *Totality and Infinity*, as denoted by the titles of these two major books. Whereas *Totality and Infinity* is a philosophical work where the relational term 'and' is central, the later work presents a philosophy of 'otherwise' and of 'beyond.' Whereas the language of *Totality and Infinity* grows from and remains committed to the in-between signified by the conjunction 'and,' the thought of *Otherwise than Being* is articulated within a space that is no longer entangled in opposites. In *Otherwise than Being*, Levinas continues the exploration of such themes as sameness and alterity, interiority and exteriority and ontology and ethics, but does so in a language that extracts itself from the fundamental tensions constitutive to the actual relationships between these terms. The language of *Otherwise than Being* no longer understands itself as located between totality *and* infinity. It is not a language of betweens, but a language aspiring to speak of transcendence beyond the burden of the finite. Is such a task possible?

The complexity of Levinas' attitude to phenomenology requires separate discussion.[12] For my current purposes, however, making two relevant points will suffice. First, Levinas' presentation of the phenomenology from which he distances himself is often surprisingly narrow. Hence, for example, in identifying phenomenology only with the noetic-noematic structuring and domination of the field of sense, Levinas chooses a dogmatic interpretation of what phenomenology can offer and of what he knows it does offer (*Otherwise than Being* was written when phenomenology had already left the Husserlian paradigm long behind).

Moreover, despite a rhetoric that is explicitly antagonistic to phenomenology, *Otherwise than Being* also harbours a few crucial, perhaps precious, moments in which his phenomenological sensitivity appears to be the driving force of his thinking and stands in opposition to his declared intentions. A moment of this kind can be found, for example, in the section on 'Saying and Subjectivity,' where Levinas introduces his philosophical project and the unique language it compels by contrasting it with phenomenological language. For him, unlike the ethical language that seeks 'to articulate the breakup of a fate that reigns in essence,'[13] phenomenology is a clear manifestation of the language of ontology that merges fully with the said: 'What does saying signify before signifying a said? Can we try to show the crux of a plot that is not reducible to phenomenology, that is, to the thematization of the said?'[14]

Levinas quite demonstratively turns his back on phenomenology. For him, phenomenology is 'the thematization of the said,' a form of reflection that can only betray 'the plot of the saying.' Yet, as he moves to explain in the very next passage, the relationship between the said and the saying, the mood and affinity of his reflection turns uniquely phenomenological:

> The plot of the saying that is absorbed in the said is not exhausted in this manifestation. It imprints its trace on the thematization itself, which hesitates between, on the one hand, structuration, order of a configuration of entities, world and history for historiographers and, on the other hand, the order of non-nominalized apophansis of the other, in which the said remains a *proposition*, a proposition made to a neighbor, 'a signifyingness dealt' (*significance baillée*) to the other. Being, the verb of a proposition, is, to be sure, a theme, but it makes essence resound without entirely deadening the echo of the saying that bears it and brings it to light.[15]

The Saying, according to Levinas, is what cannot be deduced in any a priori manner or read off a conceptual matrix. He suggests that, in order to recognize 'the plot of the saying,' an alternative perspective must be adopted, one that reveals indeterminate grounds of sense stretching in between the endpoints of what is entirely beyond language and what is entirely identical to the language of the said. The Saying is 'absorbed in the said' and, as such, it apparently cannot be distinguished from the spoken content. And yet, what attentiveness to the concreteness of the phenomenon reveals is that, while losing itself in the Said, the saying has nevertheless not disappeared: it is present in the form of the effaced.

The common internalization of the frontal's rule inevitably subordinates the saying to the said and, thereby, erases its very distinctiveness. The saying's lack of distinctiveness, however, is not indicative of its absence from the frame of the said but indicative of the fact that it cannot be framed frontally. Furthermore, if we (re) position ourselves in relation to the complexity and richness of the phenomenon of sense, we will see that the surrender of the saying to the reign of the frontal is not something that is only structurally given but is, in itself, an event that resonates, albeit in subliminal ways, within the domain of sense. Like the municipality's deliberate erasure of provocative graffiti from a public building, the erasure of the saying leaves traces too. The saying cannot appear frontally, but can reverberate as that which the frontal relegates to oblivion. The saying appears as the 'the erased,' or 'the cancelled' of the frontal: it is not part of the thematization of the said but it is present in a way that 'imprints its trace on the thematization itself.' The saying is present as a trace, as evidence of a presence that is neither full nor positive, a presence that cannot be subordinated to the question of the identity – the sameness of the existence – of the one who had been there.

> A trace is not a sign like any other. But it also plays the role of a sign; it can be taken for a sign … But when a trace is thus taken as a sign, it is exceptional with respect to other signs in that it signifies outside of every intention of signaling and

outside of every project of which it would be the aim ... Its
original signifyingness is sketched out in, for example, the
fingerprints left by someone who wanted to wipe away his
traces and carry out a perfect crime. He who left traces in
wiping out his traces did not mean to say or do anything by
the traces he left ... To be qua *leaving a trace* is to pass, to
depart, to absolve oneself.[16]

The Saying is the voice of departing, the continual departure of the
Other from the realm of the same. Poet Nathan Zach writes of his
father: 'He walked past me/ I could have touched the edges of his
overcoat/ I didn't./ Who could have/ Known what I did not know.'[17]
As in the case of Zach's father, the saying of the Other appears
within reach, within our knowing, but invariably also leaves the self
in a position of 'not touching and not knowing.' The saying is a
silent impossibility that, by its very presence, disrupts the unity and
self-identity of sense, creating spaces, unknown (unexpected and
irregular) distances within the fullness of our words.

What Levinas' optics aims to illuminate is precisely this
complex topography consisting of points of rupture, which all
remain unmarked on the map of the frontal. At the same time,
however, there is no synoptic gaze that can help us trace such a
topography because a global – necessarily external – perspective
on the landscape of language inevitably destroys the viewpoints
made possible from within the inside of language. How and where
should we position ourselves within the language we speak to allow
the oblique trajectory leading toward the Other to show itself? On
what kind of optics does a mole depend upon when moving in its
burrows? What Levinas suggests is not a kind of abstract thought
but a unique modality of vision: 'a "vision" without image, bereft
of the synoptic and totalizing objectifying virtues of vision, a
relation of an intentionality of a wholly different type.'

In many ways, there is indeed much in common here with phenomenology's unique modalities of reflection: an intentionality of
what cannot be thought, what cannot be heard or of what may

ultimately never reveal itself (e.g. the saying). This is an optics that requires patience. We need to wait and see, listen and wait, and indeed listening means being open to, laying in wait for surprises. Yet, whereas phenomenology opens up to phenomena through the 'suspension of judgment,' the 'untying of knots,' 'withdrawing from involvement,' and 'letting be,' Levinas' optics rests on a strong principle of commitment – a basic situation of obligation – to the other person. As such, it not only consists of an openness toward the unexpected, as, for example, in Gene Hackman's role as Harry Caul, a surveillance expert, in Francis Ford Coppola's *The Conversation*. Alternatively, the listening called for by Levinasian optics is of a kind whose inner form is responsibility: think here, for example, of the idiosyncratic sense of responsibility that Wiesler, the surveillance agent of the Stasi – the secret police of East Germany – develops toward the couple he spies on in Florian Henckel von Donnersmarck's film *The Lives of Others*.

In order to hear the saying of the other person, it is not enough to release it from its latency or to liberate it from its entanglement with the said. Letting the saying show itself – in the phenomenological sense of a *gelassenheit* – is not enough. The saying does not show itself and will not let itself be heard by anyone whose listening is done for the sake of listening. In fact, the very attempt to bring the saying to giving itself over to us listeners is bound to fail. The saying of the Other will never give itself, will not become a given. Quite the contrary: in order to resonate, the saying (is what) needs the giving of a listener. Its opening up to a listener is not only due to the listener's perceptive and discerning qualities but, above all, to the listener's responsibility, the readiness to respond to the other person's talk. For Levinas, the saying can reveal itself only if 'we will do and listen' (Exodus 24:7).

Talk 5
Word, Window, Screen

The word is a window; if it forms a screen, it must be rejected.

Totality and Infinity

'The word is a window' but, as implied by Levinas, it may all too often 'form a screen.' When it creates a screen, our access to the outside, to the exterior, is blocked and replaced by a virtual double, a content-bearing surface that leaves us enclosed within our selves, as if we were, without knowing, looking at a mirror. When the word is a screen, we never leave our own skins because the meaning that is offered to us is pre-framed to fit the structure of our apprehension. When the word functions as a screen, the human face is erased and its place as a foundation for the meaningful is taken up by an anonymous surface that can only give rise to frontal meaning. When the word is a screen, the 'what' of speech conceals the 'who' from which speaking emanates.

Thus, when the Other's words present us only with closed, tightly framed meanings, when the meaning of these words is given to us as a fait accompli, chances are high that the screen has taken over the field of sense, that our openness to meaning is dominated by the frontal. And yet, we should also remember that the fact of the frontal is not a coincidence; the frontal is intrinsic to the meaningfulness of language which is always on the seam – silently wavering – between the window and the screen.

The possibility of an opening of language as a window to the Other is as much part of our talk routines as that of its virtual consolidation as a screen. These possibilities are not located in different areas of language, nor do they belong to different types of discourse or to separate kinds of linguistic situations. Moreover, it is particularly wrong to understand them as depending on the character of the acquaintance or relationship, such as the closeness or distance, between speakers. The word can open up as a window in situations of strangeness, alienation, conflict of interests, disagreement or misunderstanding, just as it can turn impenetrable and create a screen between people who are close and understanding, friends or intimate partners. This complexity can be recognized only by attending to the concreteness of the linguistic phenomenon, something that writers often do better than abstract thinkers. Take the example of Milan Kundera who, in *The Unbearable Lightness of Being*,[1] makes a point of language's tendency to shut itself to the other person, and does so by locating the transformation of language into a screen in the sphere of intimacy between lovers.

'Words Misunderstood,' the third part of Kundera's book, deals with the relationship between Sabina, an exiled Czech artist living in Geneva, and her lover Franz, a university professor. Kundera describes the relationship between Franz and Sabina by creating a lexicon that compares their understanding of crucial words figuring in the everydayness of their shared world and in their lovers' discourse. Surprisingly, the 'entries' of this lexicon reveal a variety of inconsistencies, crucial discrepancies and incompatibilities that, notwithstanding the lovers' intimacy, attest to the absence of a shared grounding for their apparently meaningful interaction. The scene relevant for our purposes is one that unfolds when Franz visits Sabina's studio to invite her to come with him to Palermo. Franz, who leads a far more conservative life than Sabina, is happy with the idea of travelling with his beloved because the very distance from Geneva allows him to more easily repress the guilt of betraying his wife. '"How would you like to go to Palermo ten days from now?" asked Franz. "I prefer Geneva," she answered. She was standing in front of her easel examining a work in progress.'[2] They discuss the issue, when Sabina, 'with a curious nonchalance, as if completely unaware of Franz's presence, slowly removed her blouse.'[3] The scene proceeds as follows:

Standing there in her skirt and bra, she suddenly ... fixed Franz with a long stare. That stare bewildered him; he could not understand it. All lovers unconsciously establish their own rules of the game, which from the outset admit no transgression. The stare she had just fixed on him fell outside their rules ... It was neither provocative nor flirtatious, simply interrogative. The problem was, Franz had not the slightest notion what it was asking. Next she stepped out of her skirt and, taking Franz by the hand, turned him in the direction of a large mirror propped against the wall. Without letting go of his hand, she looked into the mirror with the same long questioning stare, training it first on herself, then on him. Near the mirror stood a wig stand with an old black bowler hat on it. She bent over, picked up the hat, and put it on her head. The image in the mirror was instantaneously transformed: suddenly it was a woman in her undergarments, a beautiful, distant, indifferent woman with a terribly out-of-place bowler hat on her head, holding the hand of a man in a gray suit and a tie. Again he had to smile at how poorly he understood his mistress. When she took her clothes off, it wasn't so much erotic provocation as an odd little caper, a happening à deux. His smile beamed understanding and consent. He waited for his mistress to respond in kind, but she did not. Without letting go of his hand, she stood staring into the mirror, first at herself then at him. The time for the happening had come and gone. Franz was beginning to feel that the caper ... had dragged on too long. So he gently took the brim of the bowler hat between two fingers, lifted it off Sabina's head with a smile, and laid it back on the wig stand ... For several more seconds she remained motionless, staring at herself in the mirror. Then Franz covered her with tender kisses and asked her once more to go with him in ten days to Palermo. This time she said yes unquestioningly, and he left. He was in an excellent mood again. Geneva, which he had cursed all his life as the metropolis of boredom, now seemed beautiful and full of adventure.[4]

Although the scene ends in mutual agreement and, to Franz's joy, with Sabina's consent to his request, at the core of the meeting is a breakdown of understanding. Sabina's behaviour, like the black bowler hat she puts on, remains an impenetrable blind spot in Franz's field of vision. The scene, which begins with the unexpected gesture of Sabina's undressing and continues with her putting on the hat in front of the mirror, reaches its end when Franz imposes closure on the situation.

Sabina's gesture opens up to meaning in several ways. On the one hand, this is an act of revelation or self-exposure whose immediate expression is the naked body. On the other, Sabina's gesture opens up as a question, a posing of a question. This questioning is unexpressed, unpronounced and remains unanswered, but it is nevertheless constantly present in the interrogative gaze Sabina fixes on Franz. We may even say that Sabina poses herself as a question to Franz. She is not only interested in the mere resonance of her question but in opening herself up as a question to the specific man looking at her. The question she asks is addressed to Franz and to him only. And its meaningfulness is thus inseparable from the horizon of Franz's presence in front of her.

For Franz, the meaning of Sabina's behaviour remains unclear. He is bewildered by the situation precisely because it seems to defy any familiar classification. In particular, he fails to make sense of the meaning of Sabina's hat and the central place it assumes in the situation. For a passing moment, Franz seems close to losing his well-tempered balance, but because he is a clever and kind person and also because he really cares about Sabina, he does not allow his uncertainty, or his momentary insecurity, to dominate his reactions. Franz does everything in his power to close the troublesome gap and push his way back to the firm ground of mutual understanding. He literally removes what he identifies as a concrete obstacle, the mark of the rift that had opened up between them, and returns the hat to its place, on the margins of the human interaction. He covers Sabina's (uncovered) body with kisses and succeeds in returning to the initial conversation about the possibility of a shared trip. Franz returns to the familiarity of everyday language, insists on the frontal, and replaces Sabina's open question with a clear, informative one: '[He] asked her once more to go with him in ten days to Palermo. This time she said yes unquestioningly, and he left.'

Whereas Franz's joy and satisfaction enable him to forget at once his inability to understand Sabina, she – remaining alone in the studio – returns immediately to the mirror and again puts on the black bowler, 'the Charlie Chaplin hat.' For Sabina, the hat is not a practical accessory, a costume, or an item of vintage clothing. The hat does not carry any standard, typical, meaning nor does it have one consistent meaning. In Sabina's world, the hat embodies, appears through, an intricate netting of personal and biographical significations that cannot be reduced to a clear functionality. The meaningfulness of the hat rests on Sabina's attachment to it or, in other words, the hat 'has a story,' a story woven into Sabina's life, her world, her temporality. Kundera describes this as follows:

> But let us return to the bowler hat. First, it was a vague reminder of a forgotten grandfather, the mayor of a small Bohemian town during the nineteenth century. Second, it was a memento of her father. After the funeral her brother appropriated all their parents' property, and she, refusing out of sovereign contempt to fight for her rights, announced sarcastically that she was taking the bowler hat as her sole inheritance. Third, it was a prop for her love games with Tomas. Fourth, it was a sign of her originality, which she consciously cultivated. She could not take much with her when she emigrated, and taking this bulky, impractical thing meant giving up other, more practical ones. Fifth, now that she was abroad, the hat was a sentimental object.[5]

The memories woven into the hat are indeed important to Sabina, but it would be wrong to understand the hat solely as a collection of discrete moments in the trajectory of her life.

The bowler hat was a motif in the musical composition that was Sabina's life. It returned again and again, each time with a different meaning, and all the meanings flowed through the bowler hat like water through a riverbed. I might call it Heraclitus' ('You can't step twice into the same river') riverbed: the bowler hat was a bed through which each time Sabina saw another river flow, another *semantic river*: each time the same object would give rise to a new meaning, though all former meanings would resonate (like an echo, like a parade of echoes) together with the new one. Each new experience would resound, each time enriching the harmony.[6]

Sabina's hat speaks to her in various voices. It is suffused with the presence of her father, her childhood, her motherland, her language, her history, her independence, her relationship with men, her singular love for Tomas, the failure of this love, her loneliness, her choices, fantasies, dreams, hopes, pride and so forth. But what makes the hat so significant, according to Kundera, is not its embodiment of a certain set of determinate and given meanings, but precisely the way in which the hat has become a channel for the flow and accumulation of ever new meanings in time. For Kundera, beside the shared and average forms of semantically structured meanings, there is a more subtle and hidden flow of meaning that is more difficult to identify. Although Franz and Sabina 'had a clear understanding of the logical meaning of the words they exchanged, they failed to hear the semantic susurrus of the river flowing through them.'[7]

Franz's failure to hear that vibration or 'susurrus' flowing through Sabina's words underscores the extent to which Sabina's words are deeply implanted in her temporality and her world and cannot therefore be understood as complete and self-sufficient constructs of sense. Like her words, the black hat too is not just another fact in her world. It is not a fully constituted object whose sense can be framed and exhausted by facticity. Instead, the bowler hat is a trace of the continual becoming – the growth and transformation

– of Sabina's world. Its meaningfulness unfolds in the tension, the mutual play between the weight of the past and the nameless openness of the future. Hence, Franz is unable to understand the place of the bowler not only because he is unfamiliar with its story but primarily because he is incapable of being part of that story. In this context, Kundera uses a musical metaphor:

> While people are fairly young and the musical composition of their lives is still in the opening bars, they can go about writing it together and exchange motifs … but if they meet when they are older, like Franz and Sabina, their musical compositions are more or less complete, and every motif, every object, every word means something different to each of them.[8]

Franz, according to Kundera, fails to make sense of the situation because Sabina's gesture, her use of the bowler hat, is a movement tied to the complexity of a complete musical composition, to which Franz has no access. He confronts an insurmountable abyss of which the hat is symbolic; a semantic river that Franz will never be able to cross.

> And so when she put on the bowler hat in his presence, Franz felt uncomfortable, as if someone had spoken to him in a language he did not know. It was neither obscene nor sentimental, merely an incomprehensible gesture. What made him feel uncomfortable was its very lack of meaning.[9]

Kundera scrutinizes the relationship between Sabina and Franz by attending to the ceaseless reverberation of difference and alterity in the midst of intimacy, showing that the more significant gaps in our understanding of others are never informational in character. A misunderstanding ensuing from misinformation is, in itself, never essential because, in principle, it can be filled. Accordingly, even if Franz could have obtained all the missing information about Sabina's life, he would have still remained deaf to the semantic susurrus resonating from Sabina's handling of her black bowler hat. What characterizes Franz's failure, then, is not lack of information but, above all, an inability to respond to the fact that he was addressed by Sabina.

On this point, however, Kundera's description might be slightly misleading. Kundera compares Franz to a person who cannot make sense of a foreign language. But is Sabina really not speaking Franz's language? Do we want to say that, beside the public language, she is also speaking another utterly private language? Would it be right to describe Franz's problematic reaction simply in terms of a cognitive failure, that is, a failure to understand a foreign language or to decipher an undisclosed code?

Indeed, Sabina makes Franz feel excluded, an outsider, a complete stranger to what has opened up between them. Yet, what he remains so alienated from is not any kind of sealed, exclusive space within which private meanings dwell. The opposite is the case: Sabina has no secret that she keeps only to herself. In the space between them all is in the open. Nothing is hidden from Franz, nothing his eyes are made not to see. What eludes him, rather, is precisely what is made for his eyes only. Franz looks at and listens to Sabina. Her behaviour surprises him. But the surprise does not lead him beyond the familiar average ways of responding to meaning. Franz wants to understand Sabina and sincerely seeks a given general pattern, a concept, a description that will enable him to determine the meaning of what he sees. But when he fails at it, and knows he has failed, he does not recognize the need for a different kind of seeing or listening. Despite his discontent, he remains committed to the general and public averageness that guides his frontal engagement with meaning. For him, understanding Sabina can only mean one thing: it means to frame and translate her intelligibility in terms already known to him – standard, common and familiar.

What Franz fails to see is that meaning has opened up between Sabina and himself in a completely singular way, in a way that dissolves when forced to meet the general and anonymous rule of informative content. Sabina's discourse does not meet the standards of frontal meaning: it is real, singular and irreplaceable. When she dons the bowler hat, Sabina does not act in terms applicable to everyone, but, at the same time, there is no way of being in her place. To put this directly, Franz does not see Sabina. He looks for and sees Sabina in a mirror showing his own reflection. He sees her through his concerns, through his wife, and it would be just as right to say that he sees her as a projection of his imagination: far from home, outside the law, beyond the realm of responsibility.

Franz, as noted, does not succeed in finding an answer – or in providing a response – to that 'long questioning stare' through which Sabina addresses him. He fails to respond to the manner Sabina addresses, faces, and turns to him, because he is deaf to the possibility that a radical alterity resonates in her *peniyya*. Is Franz a captive of that 'false romantic idea' – as Levinas calls it – that love is 'a confusion between two beings'? Or has he merely remained confined to the convenient domain of the self with its familiar meaning routines?[10] For Levinas,

> the pathos of love consists … in an insurmountable duality of beings; it is a relationship with whatever slips away. The relationship does not *ipso facto* neutralize alterity but conserves it … The other as other here is not an object which becomes our or which becomes us, to the contrary, it withdraws into its mystery.[11]

Franz respects and loves Sabina, but the frontal manner in which he looks at her, cannot allow her to remain in her alterity. Franz is a good example of a person who completely internalizes and whose experience of meaning wholly depends on the frontal nature of the gaze as its standard. As such, he relates to the appearance of meaning as if it were a given fact, a fact that fully determines the horizons of his own freedom in engaging the visual or vis-à-vis language. His internalization of a frontal picture of meaning hides from him his own freedom and thus absolves him of the very responsibility for realizing this freedom in the daily encounter with the Other. In this respect, Franz functions as the watchman of the Said, refusing, guarding against, any acknowledgement of the idiosyncratic presence of the Saying. And we may consequently say that his misunderstanding is not a cognitive failure but primarily an ethical one.

And what about Sabina? Can her Saying be listened to? What would it take to be responsive to Sabina's alterity? Where is the 'window' in her talk? Kundera, as noted, thinks of the singular meaning of Sabina's address to Franz in musical terms, somewhat resembling Wittgenstein who writes: 'Understanding a sentence is much more akin to understanding a theme in music than one may think.'[12] Elaborating on this metaphor, one could say that, when Sabina uses the motif of the bowler hat, she is not asking Franz to understand her music but rather to respond, possibly to join her in holding together what her music opens up. Franz senses that Sabina is addressing a question to him, but since her question does not resemble the standard kind of question structure that is familiar to him (for example, 'How would you like to go to Palermo?'), he does not know how to understand it.

Franz's listening allows him to hear only the Said. His way of looking allows him to see only objects and facts. But Sabina does not present him with contents that, as contents, are fully determined and complete. Franz understands that Sabina is posing a question to him, but is far from realizing that he himself is the subject of that question, that *he* is being put in question. Sabina's question, her Saying, calls Franz for a response that only he could offer. Its form is: Here I am!

Talk 6
Listening to a Big Bird

The tale of 'The Turkey Prince' by Rabbi Nahman of Bratslav goes as follows:

> Once there was a prince who went mad and imagined that he was a turkey. He undressed, sat naked under the table, and abjured all food, allowing nothing to pass his lips but a few oats and scraps of bones. His father, the king, brought all the physicians to cure him, but they were of no use.
>
> Finally, a wise man came to the king and said: I pledge to cure him.
>
> The wise man promptly proceeded to undress and sat under the table next to the prince, pecking oats and heaving at scraps of bones, which he gobbled up. The prince asked him: 'Who are you and what are you doing here?'
>
> Said the wise man: 'Who are you and what are you doing here?' The prince replied: 'I am a turkey.' To which the wise man responded: 'I am a turkey too.' So the two turkeys sat together until they became accustomed to one another. Seeing this, the wise man signaled to the king to fetch him a shirt. Putting on the shirt, he said to the prince: 'Do you really think that a turkey may not wear a shirt? Indeed he may, and that does not make him any less a turkey.' The prince was much taken by these words and also agreed to wear a shirt. At length, the wise man signaled to be brought a pair of trousers. Putting them on, he said to the prince: 'Do you

really think that a turkey is forbidden trousers? Even with
trousers on, he is perfectly capable of being a proper turkey.'
The prince acknowledged this as well, and he too put on a
pair of trousers, and it was not long before he had put on
the rest of his clothes at the wise man's directions. Following
this, the wise man asked to be served human food from the
table. He took and ate, and said to the prince: 'Do you really
think that a turkey is forbidden to eat good food? One may
eat all manner of good things and still be a proper turkey
"comme il faut."' The prince listened to him on this too, and
began eating like a human being. Seeing this, the wise man
addressed the prince: 'Do you really think that a turkey is
condemned to sit under the table? That isn't necessarily so
– a turkey also walks around any place it wants and no one
objects.' And the prince thought this through and accepted
the wise man's opinion. Once he got up and walked about
like a human being, he also began behaving like a complete
human being.[1]

For Rabbi Nahman of Bratslav, the story about the wise man
healing the prince serves as an allegory affirming the possibility
of helping those who are lost to find their way back – however far
they may have strayed – and return to 'the royal road,' to God.
This is an optimistic tale that suggests the possibility of talking
even after language has collapsed and nothing more can be said.
This possibility of responding creatively, of not surrendering to
the crisis of language is presented in the tale as essential to the
therapeutic process. The healing conversation, according to Rabbi
Nahman, is one that succeeds in spanning an abyss that, at first
glance, appears unbridgeable. The healing occurs when the prince,
with the wise man's help, crosses the bridge once again, closes the
troublesome distance and 'returns home,' to his natural place as
the king's son.

The tale's starting point is the anomalous situation – 'the
madness' – in which the prince finds himself. The prince has
changed, and this metamorphosis is a matter of grave concern to

his surroundings. What makes this change particularly disturbing is that it leads to the collapse of the shared ground, of the commonality of meaning that up to that point, had been taken completely for granted. The prince's new situation – his existence as a turkey – appears to foreclose any option of communicating with him and, in the palace, the ineffectiveness of the familiar patterns of communication is immediately interpreted as a sign of the prince's illness, his aberrance or abnormality. For the king and the doctors, the prince has become an outsider, an alien who no longer shares a standard sense of the world, who has ceased to belong to the community of the 'we.' In this respect, the attitude toward the prince is governed by the implicit presupposition that, whereas the shared world of sense is in essence uniform and homogeneous, any breakthrough of alterity, like that of the prince, is opposed to the world of sense that 'we' share. In the story, this dichotomous structure is expressed through a series of specific antitheses: human and animal, dressed and naked, being at or under the table.

Accordingly, the attempts to heal the prince rest on this opposition between the ordinary meaningfulness of the world and the prince's idiosyncratic condition. The cure that the king and the famous if unsuccessful doctors are seeking is thus one that would eliminate the strangeness that seems to exclude the prince from the domain of 'our' normal human world. That is, before the wise man comes on stage, all efforts are invested in finding a remedy that will bring the prince back to the familiar abode of ordinary everydayness: a task understood as the necessary overcoming, the erasing of the alterity that has embedded itself at the core of the prince's self-understanding.

Enter the wise man. He sees things differently and, to begin with, resists the appeal of any binary conception of the situation. The path he takes is essentially dialogical. His engagement with the prince not only develops as a dialogue, but also rests on the strong conviction that a puzzling dialogue of this kind is at all possible. The wise man, who in the palace also has the role of an Other, does not hasten to position the prince's radical alterity beyond the common horizons of shared meaning. For him, the abyss that has opened up between the prince and the community does not preclude the possibility of mutual understanding. Like the doctors, the wise man seeks to reintegrate the prince into the public domain of shared intelligibility but, unlike them, he does not envision the ideal of shared meaning as opposed to, or as excluding the prince's core of alterity.

The wise man manages to lead the prince back to the meaningfulness of ordinary everydayness, but does so without making any attempt to eliminate the prince's alterity, enabling the prince to return to his original position as prince without having to lose or renounce his identity as a turkey. Instead of struggling against the prince's birdlike predilections, the wise man endorses a pragmatic approach that allows the prince to find place, within the human context, for those singular and incommensurable aspects of his existence. As he persuades the prince to wear human clothes again, he also succeeds in bringing the prince to 'put on' a legible pattern of behaviour. The wise man helps the prince to again find a home in the public domain of human meaning but, at the same time, allows the prince to preserve the singularity that had turned him into a complete stranger. He allows the prince to be a stranger and also an insider, a 'fowly' prince or a princely fowl.

Can the Bratslav tale illuminate in any way the question of alterity's presence in language? Does it take us further in our discussion of Levinas? At first sight, the tale may not seem compatible with the insight I have tried to develop so far. Indeed, when radical alterity seems to erupt at the beginning of the story, it takes on the form of a deviant event that calls for immediate healing and for a return to the homogeneity of the same. The tale's ending seems similar in this respect, since it too marks the prince's return to the common domain of sense: the prince is cured and is fully fit to take part again in the kingdom's affairs. The disturbance that had momentarily alarmed the space of the same becomes a thing of the past. Order returns, and the law of the same continues to dominate as before.

But upon further scrutiny, things are not so simple: despite the happy resolution of the plot, the tale's ending subverts the possibility of ever returning to a simple and homogeneous form of everyday meaning. True, the prince recovers and, for his surroundings, his illness is a matter of the past, a passing affliction. His position at the centre of the public sphere is completely restored. But for us, the readers of the tale, something important has changed. Contrary to the king and his court, we cannot easily forget the eruption of that strangeness that had for a moment threatened the cohesiveness of the royal standards of the meaningful. For us, not only has that dimension of strangeness not disappeared but, in a certain sense, it has become more dominant. In regaining his stature and returning to his royal duties, the prince is a prince is a prince. Yet, as readers, we cannot ignore the fact that the prince continues to experience the world from the perspective of a big bird.

The successful return of the princely turkey to the social domain subverts the homogeneity of the shared space of sense, calling into question our trust in the very possibility of such homogeneity. The wise man enabled the prince to reintegrate into the world of shared meaning by downplaying the role of the turkey in him. But the fact that the princely turkey can feel at home in the public domain of sense – the fact that his alterity remains unidentified – attests not only to the community's blindness to his alterity but, above all, to the possibility that the turkey's unresolved presence may always silently resonate even in the most prevailing (royal) standards of human significations.

The tale thus invites us to recognize that the prince's unique existence in the space of language is, ultimately, no different from our own and from that of others. It invites us to see that a dimension of radical alterity can beat at the heart of the public meaning we share. It encourages us to question the sameness and uniformity grounding our shared space of sense, and does so by suggesting that we can never identify nor contain our interlocutor's point of entry or mode of connecting to the language he or she speaks.

Here, we are actually required to return to Levinas' optics and its suggestion that the space of language consists of invisible centres of gravity, heterogeneous and irregular inflections generated by the Other's very presence. To listen is thus to be open to an unresolved tension in the language of the other person, a tension between, on the one hand, the public uniformity of signification (a prince's words) and, on the other, the evolvement of these forms of sense rooted in the utterly foreign and inaccessible habitat of a big bird. In this context, the Levinasian image of listening to language 'as a window rather than as a screen' underscores the intersection of language and visuality. It thus evokes, again, the possibility of a new optics, inviting us to see through the determined, given, forms of sense into the anarchic unexpected fusion of prince and turkey, that is, to listen to that stridency that invariably resonates in language if we only care to respond to it.

Talk 7
The Open

Ethics is an optics. But it is a 'vision' without image, bereft
of the synoptic and totalizing objectifying virtues of vision, a
relation of an intentionality of a wholly different type.

Totality and Infinity

All is in the open (that was this work's starting point). And yet, a
fundamental dimension remains hidden. We talk. I look at your face.
I can describe or characterize it; I can draw comparisons. Yet, the very
gaze focusing so intensively on your face can easily remain blind to
it (blind to its turning, its *penniyah*, its alterity). So too concerning
your speech. I listen to you. I hear and understand what you say. I
can repeat what you say, sum it up, analyse it, ask questions about it
– and throughout remain deaf to what you say. How is that possible?
What kind of concealment is involved here? What kind of blindness?
Clearly, this is not an ordinary form of blindness in which we are
denied access to visual information. Quite the contrary. The situation
that concerns this work is, as suggested, one where the eye is flooded
with information and can see all. The contemporary eye sees – has
access to – just everything, yet something fundamental nevertheless
eludes it. How can the open – laying bare, in the clear – possibly hide?

What is at stake here is a twofold, second order, form of
concealment: not the hiddenness of any positive content – of a
'something' – but, inversely, the very appearance of visual contents
hiding a dimension of the visual that cannot be framed as content.
In other words, the kind of concealment that has concerned me
here is not one that occurs when a positive content eludes the eye
but rather the opposite – it occurs when a positive content 'seizes'
our eye, fixating it in a way that makes the eye oblivious to its
freedom and responsibility.

131

For Levinas, our prototypical ways of seeing, our basic visual routines, are a clear example of the tendency to repress the presence of the inner concealment, the fundamental invisibility reverberating within the realm of sense. Thus, as suggested, vision remains, for him a negative paradigm that should be distinguished from the discursive appearance of sense. 'Vision operates in … [a] manner totally impossible in discourse. For vision is essentially an adequation of exteriority and interiority.' That is, in vision, 'exteriority is reabsorbed in the contemplative soul as an *adequate idea*.'[1] In contradistinction, 'the exteriority of discourse cannot be converted into interiority. The interlocutor can have no place in an inwardness; he is forever outside'[2] For Levinas, discourse opens up what the gaze closes. 'Speech refuses vision, because the speaker does not deliver images of himself only, but is personally present in his speech, absolutely exterior to any image he would leave.'[3] Hence, unlike the gaze, speech always leaves a trace, always points to an exteriority that cannot be brought in.

The contrast between discourse and vision is often underscored by Levinas though, as suggested, he is also consistently concerned with an alternative order of vision, 'a "vision" without image, bereft of the synoptic and totalizing objectifying virtues of vision,' a vision that meets the speaking of the Other.

This unique mode of vision, Levinas' optics, requires an opening of the gaze to what it cannot contain, that is, to what can never become a visual content and can never be framed as an image-object: this is the absolute alterity or exteriority of the Other. For Levinas, the very existence of a radical exteriority is what enables us to go on searching and living with meaning in a world that has fully succumbed, as Baudrillard puts it, to 'the implosion of contents – the absorption of meaning.' The presence of such an exteriority is necessary as a measure for our orientation within the world of sense, as it provides a benchmark, an epitome of a distance that cannot be gathered in, that cannot be absorbed into the structure of the (personal or corporate) ego. This measure is the 'facetalk' of the other person.

And yet, as we know well, the visual is dominated today precisely by the kind of vision that is 'essentially an adequation of exteriority and interiority.' Governed by such an 'adequation,' the space of the visual cannot make room for any measure of exteriority – it relinquishes the face and talk of the Other – leaving room only for the positive contents that the gaze can frame. Once the adequation between observer and object establishes itself as the regulating measure of the gaze, what we see is always (only) what we see; and in such a context, the possibility of invisibility can only be understood in terms derivative of specific circumstances of vision that screen the appearance of what, in principle, can show itself. In an outage, we suddenly do not see one another; in the notebook, a thick marker line conceals a few written words; a heavy cloud can hide the moon; a hand blocks the camera lens. In a visual field dominated by the fit between object and consciousness, the concealment is not internal to the visual structure but rather always a circumstantial, local failure, fundamentally rectifiable. For the framing gaze, the concealed dimension of the visual is redundant and thus, with the elimination of this dimension, the visual finds itself subjugated to its virtual double. The visual becomes frontal, a screen.

The frontal, however, does not dominate the visual as an external force but belongs rather to its positive constitution. The frontal is not imposed on the visual from the outside and, as such, is not a structure from which full liberation is ever possible. At the same time, I have also argued that it is important not to accept the frontal as a complete given, a fait accompli. The relationship between the visual and the frontal is dynamic although the frontal, being a double, consistently cancels out the non-frontal possibilities of vision. Thus, one of the clear symptoms of our subjection to the frontal is the inability of *seeing otherwise* and, previous to this, of even harbouring the possibility of an alternative vision. What the frontal hides is above all the fact that the visual is not given as a fact or, in other words, that the visual is never (simply) there, *in front* of us (this is the crux of a non-frontal relation). The visual space is not made out of those slices of reality that our eyes reach out for, nor can it be understood in terms of the back screen of a collective camera obscura. Vision is not the framing of contents (objects), nor a passive givenness to the consequences of the objects' workings on the eye.

Rather, vision is, first of all, a basic form of human existence, of our being in the world, among people, among things, always already within horizons of meaning and contexts of signification. At the same time, however, in being visual, we are never in a position in which meaning is *there* in our hands, fully given to us. The visuality of the world is not simply one more fact in our world but always an integral part of the complex structure of our dwelling in it. Seeing is being seen. And being in the world involves living that intersection of vision and visibility, that is, living as part of a visual space whose characteristics are intimately tied to who we are. Yet, to repeat, the meaning of who-we-are is not a given fact but, as Levinas argues, an open question, the answer to which cannot be given in general because it already assumes the particular form of a response to the turning, the *peniyyah* of the Other.

The turning of the Other is a vector essential to the visual field and yet, under the reign of the frontal, it is levelled out, leaving a mere trace in the form of its disappearance. Hence, the call for opening up the gaze to the Other is, always, also a call for dissent, for a subversion of the rule of the frontal, for an opposition that may lack real demolition powers but is able to set off microscopic perturbations. Thus, in addressing the Other, the apparent neutrality of the visual space immediately dissolves, revealing a constitution that is neither Euclidean nor homogeneous but real and irregular in its morphology. It unfolds, as noted, in the midst of constantly changing horizons, through the topological inflection and intertwining of layers, a multiplicity of gravitation centres, surprising crevices, twists, enclosures and folds that are not given in any a priori manner – that are never there in advance – but that reveal themselves only in and through the specificity of the trajectories, structures, encounters, and interactions comprising our lives. In this sense, the visual is always pervaded by dimensions of invisibility. The visual is a domain of presentation – a making present – that, as such, necessarily involves also the unpresentable. What is visually disclosed may, surprisingly, also hide. Yet, as suggested, what is hidden by this concealment is not something that can, in principle become visible to the eye. The opening of the visual space is inseparable from a dimension that refuses to be brought to the open, that is, the projection of alterity onto the visual.

Alterity calls for a kind of vision that digs under the fully constituted image, that unravels the 'forefront' texture that meets the eye so as to disclose the non-optic core of the visual object. Thus, responding to the claim of alterity depends on the ability to identify at the core of the visual those irregular areas of impenetrability that present themselves to the eye as the unlit side of the visible, that is, as a dimension that can only be seen by resisting the laws of light or the game-rules of light (optics in its usual sense) as the name of the game.

Here, however, it would be wrong to interpret Levinas' move as an expression of that alternative modernist tradition working against the eye's satisfaction and embodying what Rosalind Krauss, in the wake of Walter Benjamin, calls 'the optical unconscious.'[4] Indeed, Levinas clearly opposes the optical framework that the frontal regulates. Yet, contrary to Krauss, he has no interest in the non-optical as a conceptual or dialectical structure. Unlike Krauss, for example, who deals with the unframable in terms of the Lacanian notion of the 'real,' structural arguments about the non-optical are, in themselves, of no concern to Levinas, who grapples with the very opening of the concrete itself.

Nevertheless, and despite the apparent similarity, Levinas' concern with the invisible ultimately differs from phenomenology as well. For Levinas, the phenomenological attempt to follow – like Merleau-Ponty – the irregular traces that the invisible leaves on the visible is, in itself, not enough in order to genuinely see otherwise, through and beyond the image. The 'wholly different type' of vision that concerns him, the vision of the Other, is one that redefines the field that the gaze firmly fixes and keeps in balance. Unlike phenomenology, however, for Levinas the need to transform or refresh the routines of the gaze is not understood in terms of the need to deepen and enrich our visual sensibilities, suspend the image, or release the eye's fixation on the object. These strategies would ultimately remain for him aesthetic exercises.

The breakdown of the frontal, the power to traverse it, is only possible through the realization of a more basic relationship with what is beyond the frontal, with what the frontal knows nothing about: 'a duty that did not ask for consent, that came into me traumatically, from beneath all rememberable present, an-archically, without beginning.'[5] The subversion of the frontal, in other words, requires no more than the most elementary of gestures: 'from self to Other'; not a mode of thinking or observation, no inner intention but responsibility – a going toward, being for the Other, responding to his or her turning, his or her face – giving. Only in the giving do we uncover that

> sign made of the very donation of the sign ... the signified sign without figure, without presence, outside the acquired, outside of civilization ... like a sound audible only in its echo, delivered to the ear without taking satisfaction in the energy of its repercussion.[6]

The giving to another person is the place where the open is revealed.

Notes

Preface: The Rule of the Frontal

1. Plato, *Phaedrus*, p. 227a.
2. Jean Baudrillard, *Simulacra and Simulation*, trans. Sheila Faria Glaser (Ann Arbor, MI: University of Michigan Press, 1994), pp. 29–30.
3. Ibid., p. 30.
4. Ibid., p. 159.
5. On the one hand, the threshold of horror and violence presented on the screens has risen and, on the other, the ghastly image (or, rather, one that is critical, didactic, artistic and so forth) is presented to us in a way that invariably takes into account the consumer structure of the eye, the need, as Susan Sontag writes, 'to arouse and to satiate' its chronic hunger.

> Image-glut keeps attention light, mobile, relatively indifferent to content. Image-flow precludes a privileged image. The whole point ... is that it is normal to switch channels, to become restless, bored. Consumers droop. They need to be stimulated, jump-started, again and again.

> Susan Sontag, *Regarding the Pain of Others* (New York: Picador, 2004), p. 106.

6.   Baudrillard, *Simulacra and Simulation*, p. 87.
7.   Ibid., pp. 81–3.
8.   Ibid., p. 164.
9.   Emmanuel Levinas, *Ethics and Infinity: Conversations with Philipe Nemo*, trans. Richard A. Cohen (Pittsburgh, PA: Duquesne University Press, 1985), p. 87.

Ethics is an Optics: Preliminary Remarks

1.   Emmanuel Levinas, 'Philosophy and the Idea of Infinity,' in *Collected Philosophical Papers*, trans. Alphonso Lingis (Pittsburgh, PA: Duquesne University Press, 1987), p. 50.
2.   Emmanuel Levinas, *Totality and Infinity*, trans. Alphonso Lingis (Pittsburgh, PA: Duquesne University Press, 2001), p. 43.
3.   Levinas, 'Philosophy and the Idea of Infinity,' p. 48.
4.   Ibid.
5.   Ibid.
6.   These are the questions discussed, for instance, in Section Two, 'Interiority and Economy,' of *Totality and Infinity*.
7.   Levinas, 'Philosophy and the Idea of Infinity,' p. 48.
8.   Ibid., pp. 48–9.
9.   Levinas, *Totality and Infinity*, p. 44.
10. Ibid., p. 43.
11. Levinas' critique of the philosophy of the same, then, does not target any particular philosophical stance but seeks to deal with the roots of our most banal existence. Hence, it appears that liberation from the philosophy of the same cannot remain merely theoretical. The possibility of opening up to the Other's alterity cannot be examined only within the new philosophical *Weltanschauung* because it is apparently related to an essential change in our patterns of selfhood.
12. In this regard, Levinas is different, for instance, from Heidegger who, besides his general rhetoric on the

forgetfulness of being, also offers detailed readings of moments he considers critical for the understanding of that forgetfulness in the history of philosophy.

13. This problematic is already incisively illuminated in Jacques Derrida's seminal article on Levinas, 'Violence and Metaphysics,' which is largely responsible for the introduction of Levinas into contemporary philosophical discourse.
14. Levinas, *Totality and Infinity*, p. 23.
15. Ibid., p. 22.
16. Ibid., p. 29.
17. Emmanuel Levinas, *Discovering Existence with Husserl*, trans. Richard A. Cohen and Michael B. Smith (Evanston, IL: Northwestern University Press, 1998), p. 13.
18. Ibid.
19. Levinas, *Totality and Infinity*, p. 28.
20. Ibid., p. 27.
21. René Descartes, *Meditations on First Philosophy*, trans. John Cottingham (Cambridge: Cambridge University Press, 1986).
22. Levinas, 'Philosophy and the Idea of Infinity,' p. 54.
23. Levinas, *Totality and Infinity*, p. 27.
24. Levinas, 'Philosophy and the Idea of Infinity,' p. 56.
25. Ibid., pp. 57–8.
26. Ibid., p. 58.

Face

Face 1: The Gleam of Infinity

1. Emmanuel Levinas, *Totality and Infinity*, trans. Alphonso Lingis (Pittsburgh, PA: Duquesne University Press, 2001), p. 24.
2. Ibid.
3. Ibid., p. 187.

Face 2: How a Face Looks

1. Emmanuel Levinas, *Ethics and Infinity*, trans. Richard A. Cohen (Pittsburgh, PA: Duquesne University Press, 1985), p. 85.
2. Ibid., pp. 85–6.
3. Emmanuel Levinas, *Totality and Infinity*, trans. Alphonso Lingis (Pittsburgh, PA: Duquesne University Press, 2001), p. 191.
4. Ibid.
5. Emmanuel Levinas, 'Meaning and Sense,' in *Collected Philosophical Papers*, trans. Alphonso Lingis (Pittsburgh, PA: Duquesne University Press, 1987), p. 95.
6. Levinas, *Ethics and Infinity*, p. 86.
7. Ibid.
8. Levinas, *Totality and Infinity*, p. 187.

Face 3: Face and Object

1. Emmanuel Levinas, 'Meaning and Sense,' in *Collected Philosophical Papers*, trans. Alphonso Lingis (Pittsburgh, PA: Duquesne University Press, 1987), p. 96.
2. Leon Battista Alberti, 'On Painting' (Book I) in *On Painting and Sculpture*, trans. Cecil Grayson (London: Phaidon, 1972), pp. 55–9.
3. Levinas' debt to and critique of Buber shows itself in a variety of Levinasian texts. The most thematic presentation can be found in Emmanuel Levinas, 'Martin Buber and the Theory of Knowledge,' in *Proper Names*, trans. Michael. B. Smith (Stanford, CA: Stanford University Press, 1996).
4. Levinas, 'Meaning and Sense,' p. 104.

Face 5: Vision, Gaze, Other

1. Edmund Husserl, *Cartesian Meditations: An Introduction to Phenomenology*, trans. Dorion Cairns (The Hague: Martinus Nijhoff, 1960), p. 89.
2. Ibid.
3. Ibid., p. 90.
4. Ibid., p. 148.
5. Ibid., pp. 148–9.
6. On Husserl's discussion of the 'inverse movement' that ultimately leads to the 'explosion' of the noematic structure, see Hagi Kenaan, 'Subject to Error: Rethinking Husserl's Phenomenology of Misperception,' *International Journal of Philosophical Studies*, 7 (1999): 55–67.
7. Emmanuel Levinas, 'Meaning and Sense,' in *Collected Philosophical Papers*, trans. Alphonso Lingis (Pittsburgh, PA: Duquesne University Press, 1987), pp. 96–7.
8. Jean-Paul Sartre, *Being and Nothingness: An Essay on Phenomenological Ontology*, trans. Hazel E. Barnes (New York: Philosophical Library, 1956), p. 233.
9. Ibid., p. 253.
10. Ibid., p. 235.
11. Ibid., p. 475.
12. Ibid., p. 364.
13. Ibid., p. 363.
14. Ibid., p. 302.
15. Ibid., p. 364.
16. Emmanuel Levinas, *Totality and Infinity*, trans. Alphonso Lingis (Pittsburgh, PA: Duquesne University Press, 2001), p. 303.
17. Emmanuel Levinas, 'Philosophy and the Idea of Infinity,' in *Collected Philosophical Papers*, trans. Alphonso Lingis (Pittsburgh, PA: Duquesne University Press, 1987), p. 55.

Face 6: Face and Resistance

1. Emmanuel Levinas, *Totality and Infinity*, trans. Alphonso Lingis (Pittsburgh, PA: Duquesne University Press, 2001), p. 28.
2. Emmanuel Levinas, *Ethics and Infinity*, trans. Richard A. Cohen (Pittsburgh, PA: Duquesne University Press, 1985), p. 86.
3. Ibid., p. 87.
4. Ibid., p. 89.
5. Emmanuel Levinas, 'Philosophy and the Idea of Infinity,' in *Collected Philosophical Papers*, trans. Alphonso Lingis (Pittsburgh, PA: Duquesne University Press, 1987), p. 55.
6. Ibid.
7. Jean-Paul Sartre, *Being and Nothingness: An Essay on Phenomenological Ontology*, trans. Hazel E. Barnes (New York: Philosophical Library, 1956), p. 222.
8. Ibid., p. 58.
9. Levinas, *Totality and Infinity*, p. 197.
10. Levinas, 'Philosophy and the Idea of Infinity,' p. 58.
11. Ibid.
12. Levinas, *Totality and Infinity*, p. 43.
13. Ibid., p. 171.
14. Emmanuel Levinas, 'Nonintentional Consciousness,' in *Entre Nous-On Thinking-of-the-Other*, trans. Michael B. Smith and Barbara Harshav (London: Athlone Press, 1998), p. 129.
15. Levinas, 'Philosophy and the Idea of Infinity,' p. 50.
16. Ibid.
17. Ibid., p. 48.
18. Ibid., p. 50.
19. Ludwig Wittgenstein, *Philosophical Investigations*, trans. G. E. M. Anscombe (New York: Macmillan, 1953), sec. 114, p. 48.
20. Emmanuel Levinas, 'Meaning and Sense,' in *Collected Philosophical Papers*, trans. Alphonso Lingis (Pittsburgh, PA: Duquesne University Press, 1987), pp. 96–7.

21. Emmanuel Levinas, 'God and Philosophy,' in *Collected Philosophical Papers*, trans. Alphonso Lingis (Pittsburgh, PA: Duquesne University Press, 1987), pp. 167–8. In another formulation: 'The "absolutely other" is not reflected in consciousness. It resists it to the extent that even its resistance is not convertible into a content of consciousness.' Levinas, 'Meaning and Sense,' p. 91.
22. Levinas, *Ethics and Infinity*, p. 96.
23. Levinas, 'Meaning and Sense,' p. 91.
24. Ibid.
25. In another formulation:

> Before the neighbor I am summoned and do not just appear; from the first I am answering to an assignation. Already the stony core of my substance is dislodged. But the responsibility to which I am exposed in such a passivity does not apprehend me as an interchangeable thing, for here no one can be substituted for me (Levinas, 'God and Philosophy,' p. 167).

Talk

Talk 1: The Face of Language

1. Emmanuel Levinas, *Totality and Infinity*, trans. Alphonso Lingis (Pittsburgh, PA: Duquesne University Press, 2001), p. 127.
2. Ibid., p. 66.
3. Maurice Merleau-Ponty, 'Eye and Mind,' trans. Carleton Dallery, in *The Primacy of Perception* (Evanston, IL: Northwestern University Press, 1964), pp. 159–90.
4. Levinas, *Totality and Infinity*, p. 66.
5. Emmanuel Levinas, 'Philosophy and the Idea of Infinity,' in *Collected Philosophical Papers*, trans. Alphonso Lingis (Pittsburgh, PA: Duquesne University Press, 1987), p. 55.

6.   Ibid.
7.   Emmanuel Levinas, 'Language and Proximity,' in *Collected Philosophical Papers*, trans. Alphonso Lingis (Pittsburgh, PA: Duquesne University Press, 1987), p. 119.
8.   Ibid., p. 121.
9.   Ibid., p. 119.
10. Emmanuel Levinas, 'Phenomenon and Enigma,' in *Collected Philosophical Papers*, trans. Alphonso Lingis (Pittsburgh, PA: Duquesne University Press, 1987), p. 70.
11. Yehuda Amichai, 'I Lost my ID' (in Hebrew), *The Hour of Grace* (Tel Aviv: Schocken, 1982), p. 40.
12. Levinas, *Totality and Infinity*, p. 171.

Talk 2: Expression

1.   Emmanuel Levinas, 'Philosophy and the Idea of Infinity,' in *Collected Philosophical Papers*, trans. Alphonso Lingis (Pittsburgh, PA: Duquesne University Press, 1987), p. 55.
2.   Emmanuel Levinas, *Totality and Infinity*, trans. Alphonso Lingis (Pittsburgh, PA: Duquesne University Press, 2001), p. 202.
3.   Ibid., p. 201.

Talk 3: The First Word

1.   Donald Woods Winnicott, *Playing and Reality* (London: Routledge, 1971).
2.   Emmanuel Levinas, *Totality and Infinity*, trans. Alphonso Lingis (Pittsburgh, PA: Duquesne University Press, 2001), p. 155.
3.   Ibid., p. 207.
4.   Ibid., p. 262.

Talk 4: Saying and Betraying

1. Emmanuel Levinas, *Otherwise than Being or Beyond Essence*, trans. Alphonso Lingis (Pittsburgh, PA: Duquesne University Press, 1998), p. 7.
2. Emmanuel Levinas, 'Language and Proximity,' in *Collected Philosophical Papers*, trans. Alphonso Lingis (Pittsburgh, PA: Duquesne University Press, 1987), p. 69.
3. Levinas, *Otherwise than Being*, p. 9.
4. Ibid., p. 6.
5. Ibid., p. 5.
6. Ibid., p. 10.
7. 'Introduction,' in *The Cambridge Companion to Levinas*, eds, Simon Critchley and Robert Bernasconi (Cambridge: Cambridge University Press, 2002), pp. 18–19. Simon Critchley's *The Ethics of Deconstruction: Derrida and Levinas* (Oxford: Blackwell, 1992) is widely considered the first book to make this connection.
8. Critchley and Bernasconi, 'Introduction,' p. 19.
9. For readings that are attracted to but ultimately resist the performative, see Bernhard Waldendfels, 'Levinas on the Saying and the Said,' in *Addressing Levinas*, eds, Eric Sean Nelson, Antje Kapust and Ken Still (Evanston, IL: Northwestern University Press, 2005). See also, Adriaan Peperzak, 'Presentation,' in *Re-Reading Levinas*, eds, Robert Bernasconi and Simon Critchley (Bloomington, IN: Indiana University Press, 1991).
10. For a critical discussion of this metaphysical picture of language see Hagi Kenaan, *The Present Personal: Philosophy and the Hidden Face of Language* (New York: Columbia University Press, 2005).
11. Levinas' critique rests on a more general move avoiding the distinction between representation and action, between the theoretical and the practical. In his view, the distinction

comes to the fore in the controversy between two key positions in the background of his writing: that of Husserl and, by contrast, that of Heidegger.

12. On the tension between two kinds of philosophical vision in *Otherwise than Being*, see Hagi Kenaan, 'The Plot of the Saying,' *Études Phénoménologiques*, vol. xxii, No. 43–44 (2006): 75–93.

13. Levinas, *Otherwise than Being*, p. 8.

14. Ibid., p. 46.

15. Ibid., pp. 46–7.

16. Emmanuel Levinas, 'Meaning and Sense,' in *Collected Philosophical Papers*, trans. Alphonso Lingis (Pittsburgh, PA: Duquesne University Press, 1987), pp. 104–5.

17. Nathan Zach, 'A Moment Please' (in Hebrew), *Various Poems* (Tel Aviv: Hakibbutz Hameuchad, 1979), p. 29.

Talk 5: Word, Window, Screen

1. Milan Kundera, *The Unbearable Lightness of Being*, trans. Michael Henry Heim (London: Faber and Faber, 1984).

2. Ibid., p. 82.

3. Ibid., p. 84.

4. Ibid., pp. 84–5.

5. Ibid., p. 87.

6. Ibid., p. 88.

7. Ibid.

8. Ibid., pp. 88–9.

9. Ibid., p. 88.

10. Emmanuel Levinas, *Ethics and Infinity*, trans. Richard A. Cohen (Pittsburgh, PA: Duquesne University Press, 1985), p. 66.

11. Ibid., p. 67.

12. Ludwig Wittgenstein, *Philosophical Investigations*, trans. G. E. M. Anscombe (New York: Macmillan, 1953), #527.

Talk 6: Listening to a Big Bird

1. 'The Turkey Prince (The Man who Became a Turkey),' trans. Lewis Glinert, http://www.dartmouth.edu/~chasidic/hebrew/rabbi_tp.html.

Talk 7: The Open

1. Emmanuel Levinas, *Totality and Infinity*, trans. Alphonso Lingis (Pittsburgh, PA: Duquesne University Press, 2001), p. 295.
2. Ibid.
3. Ibid., p. 296.
4. Rosalind Krauss, *The Optical Unconscious* (Cambridge, MA: MIT Press, 1993).
5. Emmanuel Levinas, *Humanism of the Other*, trans. Nidra Poller (Chicago, IL: University of Illinois Press, 2005), p. 7.
6. Ibid., pp. 8–9.

Index